KNIT NORO
ACCESSORIES

KNIT NORO
ACCESSORIES
30 COLORFUL
LITTLE KNITS

sixth&spring books
NEW YORK

sixth&spring books
161 Avenue of the Americas
New York, New York 10013
sixthandspringbooks.com

Managing Editor	**WENDY WILLIAMS**
Senior Editor	**MICHELLE BREDESON**
Art Director	**DIANE LAMPHRON**
Yarn Editor	**RENEE LORION**
Instructions Editor	**PAT HARSTE**
Instructions Proofreaders	**AMY POLCYN**
	JUDITH S. SLOAN
Technical Illustrations	**BARBARA KHOURI**
Photography	**ROSE CALLAHAN**
Stylist and Bookings Manager	**SARAH LIEBOWITZ**
Hair and Makeup	**INGEBORG K.**

KNIT NORO: Accessories
30 Colorful Little Knits
Sixth&Spring Books

**Library of Congress Cataloging-in-Publication Data
available upon request.**

ISBN 13: 978-1-936096-20-6

Manufactured in China
3 5 7 9 10 8 6 4 2
First Edition

Vice President, Publisher	**TRISHA MALCOLM**
Creative Director	**JOE VIOR**
Production Manager	**DAVID JOINNIDES**
President	**ART JOINNIDES**

CONTENTS

INTRODUCTION

In *Knit Noro*, some of today's top knitwear designers created a stunning
collection of cardigans, shawls, tunics and afghans, as well as accessories.
In *Knit Noro: Accessories*, small projects take center stage. Numerous designs
for scarves, hats, mittens and bags, as well as fun items like leg warmers,
an iPad sleeve and a tea cozy bring to life the beauty of Noro yarns.

For more than forty years, Eisaku Noro has been producing yarns in the
Aichi province of Japan. Made with the finest natural materials and dyed
exclusively by hand, Noro yarns are cherished by knitters all over the world.
The most notable characteristic of Noro yarns is by far their dazzling color
combinations, which range from rich jewel tones to warm and earthy hues
to eclectic acid tones. The patterns in this artful collection make use of
several Noro yarns: Iro, Kochoran, Kogarashi, Kureyon, Silk Garden, Silk
Garden Sock and Taiyo.

Because each of the projects uses only a few hanks or skeins of yarn, you
can feel free to play with and explore the entire spectrum of Noro colors.
Knit a design in the designated color for yourself, then knit another for a
friend in her favorite colorway. The possibilities are endless.

The projects in *Knit Noro: Accessories* are small, but they are not short
on design innovation or creativity. Anna Al's puzzle scarf takes a simple
motif and turns it every which way to create a stunning adornment. Cheryl
Murray's autumn sampler tote features no fewer than eight stitch patterns
knit in warm, earthy tones. Amy Polcyn's scale-pattern mitts knit in vibrant
pinks, yellows and blues will add a bright punch of color to any winter
wardrobe. Jacqueline van Dillen takes the traditional earflap hat and turns
it on its "ear" by knitting it in lace. Even the family pooch gets to enjoy
wearing Noro yarns in Astor Tsang's dog sweater.

All of these exquisite knits and many more prove yet again how versatile
and appealing Noro yarns really are.

THE PROJECTS

Puzzle Scarf

Puzzle Scarf

U-shaped motifs are knit separately and pieced together to create this lovely and enigmatic wrap.

Designed by Anna Al

Skill Level: ■■■□

Materials

- 4 1¾oz/50g skeins (each approx 110 yd/100m) of Noro *Silk Garden* (silk/kid mohair/lamb's wool) in #301 royal/purple/fuchsia/lime
- One pair size 7 (4.5mm) needles OR SIZE TO OBTAIN GAUGE

Size

Instructions are written for one size.

Knitted Measurements

Approx 8¼" x 62"/21cm x 157.5cm

Gauge

18 sts and 34 rows to 4"/10cm over garter st (knit every row) using size 7 (4.5mm) needles.
One motif measures 4" x 4"/10cm x 10cm using size 7 (4.5mm) needles.
TAKE TIME TO CHECK GAUGE.

Motif (make 30)

Cast on 37 sts.
Row 1 and all WS rows Knit.
Row 2 K14, work (k1, yo, k1) in next st, k7, work (k1, yo, k1) in next st, k14— 41 sts.
Row 4 K15, work (k1, yo, k1) in next st, k9, work (k1, yo, k1) in next st, k15— 45 sts.
Row 6 K16, work (k1, yo, k1) in next st, k11, work (k1, yo, k1) in next st, k16— 49 sts.
Row 8 K17, work (k1, yo, k1) in next st, k13, work (k1, yo, k1) in next st, k17— 53 sts.
Row 10 K18, work (k1, yo, k1) in next st, k15, work (k1, yo, k1) in next st, k18— 57 sts. Bind off knitwise.

Finishing

Block motifs lightly to measurements. Sew motifs tog foll diagram, rep rows 1–3 five times. Block assembled scarf lightly to measurements. ■

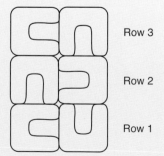

Row 3

Row 2

Row 1

Random Cable Mitts

Random Cable Mitts

Knitter's choice! A cabled rib pattern in which you decide where to work the twists results in mitts that are truly one of a kind.

Designed by Debbie O'Neill

Skill Level: ■■■□

Materials

- 1 3½oz/100g skein (each approx 328 yd/300m) of Noro *Silk Garden Sock Yarn* (lamb's wool/silk/nylon/kid mohair) in #264 tan/green/blue
- One set (5) size 2 (2.75mm) double-pointed needles (dpns) OR SIZE TO OBTAIN GAUGE
- Cable needle (cn)
- Stitch markers
- Contrasting yarn (waste yarn)

Sizes

Instructions are written for size Small. Changes for Medium and Large are in parentheses.

Knitted Measurements

Hand circumference 7 (7¾, 8¾)"/18 (19.5, 22)cm
Length of cuff approx 6"/15cm

Gauges

28 sts and 42 rnds to 4"/10cm over St st using size 2 (2.75mm) dpns.
37 sts and 42 rnds to 4"/10cm over k2, p2 rib using size 2 (2.75mm) dpns. TAKE TIME TO CHECK GAUGES.

Notes

1) Cuffs and back of hands are worked in random cable rib.
2) Palms and thumbs are worked in St st (knit every rnd).

Stitch Glossary

6-st RC Sl next 4 sts to cn and hold to *back*, k2, then p2, k2 from cn.

Random Cable Rib

Work in k2, p2 rib, working a 6-st RC as desired. (Mitts shown have only one cable per rnd and cables were worked every 2–6 rnds.) It is not necessary to keep track of what is done on right mitt in order to knit left mitt, as mitts are not intended to match.

Right Mitt

Cuff

Cast on 56 (64, 72) sts. Divide sts over 4 needles. Join and pm taking care not to twist sts on needles. Work in k2, p2 rib for at least 3 rnds before beg random cable rib. Cont in random cable rib until piece measures 6"/15cm from beg.

Establish pat sts

Next 7 rnds K13 (15, 17), work in random cable rib as established over 30 (34, 38) sts, k13 (15, 17).

Thumb gusset

Inc rnd 1 K13 (15, 17), work in random cable rib over next 30 (34, 38) sts, k1, pm, M1, k1, M1, pm, k11 (13, 15)—58 (66, 74) sts (3 sts between gusset markers). Work next rnd even.
Inc rnd 2 K13 (15, 17), work in random cable rib over next 30 (34, 38) sts, k1, sl marker, M1, knit to next marker, M1, sl marker, k11 (13, 15)—60 (68, 76) sts (5 sts between gusset markers). Work next rnd even. Rep last 2 rnds 8 times more—76 (84, 92) sts (21 sts between gusset markers).

Next rnd K13 (15, 17), work in random cable rib over next 30 (34, 38) sts, k1, place next 21 sts on waste yarn for thumb (dropping markers), cast on 3 sts, k11 (13, 15)—58 (66, 74) sts.

Hand
Next rnd K13 (15, 17), work in random cable rib over next 30 (34, 38) sts, knit to end of rnd. Cont as established until piece measures 10½"/ 26.5cm from beg. Bind off in pat sts.

Thumb
Place 21 thumb gusset sts over 2 needles.
Next rnd Join yarn and knit across sts, then with 3rd needle pick up and k 3 sts along cast-on sts of hand—24 sts. Divide sts evenly over 3 dpns. Join and pm for beg of rnds.
Rnds 1 and 2 Knit.
Rnd (dec) 3 Ssk, knit to 3 sts before marker, end k2tog, k1—22 sts. Rep rnds 1–3 once more—20 sts. Knit next 2 rnds. Bind off knitwise.

Left Mitt
Cuff
Work same as right mitt.

Establish pat sts
Next 7 rnds K13 (15, 17), work in random cable rib as established over 30 (34, 38) sts, k13 (15, 17).

Thumb gusset
Inc rnd 1 K11 (13, 15), pm, M1, k1, M1, pm, k1, work in random cable rib over next 30 (34, 38) sts, k13 (15, 17)—58 (66, 74) sts (3 sts between gusset markers). Work next rnd even.
Inc rnd 2 K11 (13, 15), sl marker, M1, knit to next marker, M1, sl marker, k1, work in random cable rib over next 30 (34, 38) sts, k13 (15, 17)—60 (68, 76) sts (5 sts between gusset markers). Work next rnd even. Rep last 2 rnds 8 times more—76 (84, 92) sts (21 sts between gusset markers).
Next rnd K11 (13, 15), place next 21 sts on waste yarn for thumb (dropping markers), cast on 3 sts, k1, work in random cable rib over next 30 (34, 38) sts, k13 (15, 17)—58 (66, 74) sts.

Hand
Next rnd K15 (17, 19), work in random cable rib over next 30 (34, 38) sts, knit to end of rnd. Cont as established until piece measures 10¼"/26.5cm from beg. Bind off in pat sts.

Thumb
Work same as right mitt. ■

Reversible Scarves

Reversible Scarves

Quadruple your fun by knitting two of these versatile scarves using two different pairs of colorways.

Designed by Karen Baumer

Skill Level: ■■■■

Materials

- 1 1¾oz/50g skein (approx 110 yd/100m) of Noro *Kureyon* (wool) each in #188 moss/purple/navy (A) and #258 black/olive/lavender (B) [shown on pages 18 and 19] OR #221 olive/hunter/purple/pink (A) and #264 hot pink/lilac/brown/purple (B) [shown above and on opposite page]
- Size 4 (3.5mm) circular needle, 24"/61cm long, OR SIZE TO OBTAIN GAUGE

Size

Instructions are written for one size.

Knitted Measurements

Approx 5¾" x 55½"/14.5cm x 140cm

Gauges

16 sts and 22 rows to 4"/10cm over reversible pat st using size 4 (3.5mm) circular needle (before blocking).
14 sts and 16 rows to 4"/10cm over reversible pat st using size 4 (3.5mm) circular needle (after blocking).
TAKE TIME TO CHECK GAUGES.

Stitch Glossary

ssyo Sl st purlwise, and at the same time, yarn over the st (from *front* to *back*). This st is treated as one st.
kssyo Knit the ssyo from the previous row, treating it as one st.
pssyo Purl the ssyo from the previous row, treating it as one st.

Reversible Pattern Stitch

(over an even number of sts)
Row 1 (RS) With A, *kssyo, ssyo; rep from * to end. Slide sts back to opposite end of needle.
Row 2 (RS) With B, *ssyo, kssyo; rep from * to end. Turn work.
Row 3 (WS) With A, *ssyo, pssyo; rep from * to end. Slide sts back to opposite end of needle.
Row 4 (WS) With B, *pssyo, ssyo; rep from * to end. Turn work.
Rep rows 1–4 for reversible pat st.

Scarf

With A, cast on 20 sts loosely.
Set-up row 1 (WS) With A, *ssyo, p1; rep from * to end. Slide sts back to opposite end of needle.
Set-up row 2 (WS) With B, *pssyo, ssyo; rep from * to end. Turn work. Cont in reversible pat st until piece measures approx 48"/122cm from beg or until there is only enough yarn rem to work 2 more RS rows, end with a WS row. Bind off loosely knitwise using A.

Finishing

With WS facing, steam-block piece to measurements. ■

Entrelac iPad Cover

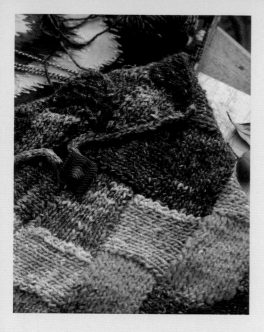

Entrelac iPad Cover

Combine Old World craft with new technology by knitting a colorful cozy for your latest gadget.

Designed by Loretta Dachman

Skill Level: ■■■■

Materials
- 1 3½oz/100g skein (each approx 220 yd/200m) of Noro *Taiyo* (cotton/silk/wool/nylon) in #10 royal/fuchsia/teal
- One pair size 7 (4.5mm) needles OR SIZE TO OBTAIN GAUGE
- Two size 7 (4.5mm) double-pointed needles (dpns) for I-cord strap)
- One 1"/25mm button
- Matching sewing thread

Size
Instructions are written for one size.

Knitted Measurements
Approx 8" x 10½"/20.5cm x 26.5cm (closed)

Gauge
17 sts and 24 rows to 4"/10cm over St st (knit on RS, purl on WS) using size 7 (4.5mm) needles. TAKE TIME TO CHECK GAUGE.

Note
Front, back and flap are made in one piece.

Stitch Glossary
kf&b Inc 1 by knitting into the front and back of the next st.

iPad Cover
Cast on 27 sts. Work in entrelac pat as foll:

Base triangles
*Row 1 (WS) P2; turn.
Row 2 K2; turn.
Row 3 P3; turn.
Row 4 K3; turn. Cont in this way, working 1 more st at end of *every* WS row until row 15 is worked as foll: P9; *do not turn*. Rep from * twice more—3 triangles completed. Turn.

Right-Side Tier
Right-hand corner triangle
Row 1 (RS) K2; turn.
Row 2 P2; turn.
Row 3 Kf&b, ssk; turn.
Row 4 P3; turn.
Row 5 Kf&b, k1, ssk; turn.
Row 6 P4; turn. Cont to inc 1 at beg of *every* RS row and work 1 more st before dec, until row 15 is worked as foll: Kf&b, k6, ssk; *do not turn*. The right-hand corner triangle is completed. Leave 9 sts on RH needle.

Right-side rectangle
Pick-up row (RS) Pick up and k 9 sts evenly spaced along edge of

next triangle (or rectangle on the foll rows); turn.

Row 1 (WS) P9, turn.

Row 2 K8, ssk (with last st of rectangle and first st of next triangle, or rectangle); turn. Rep rows 1 and 2 eight times more. *Do not turn* at end of last row. One right-side rectangle completed. Rep right-side rectangle once more—2 right-side rectangles completed.

Left-hand corner triangle

Pick-up row (RS) Pick up and k 9 sts evenly spaced along edge of last triangle (or rectangle on the foll rows); turn.

Row 1 P2tog, p7; turn.

Row 2 K8; turn.

Row 3 P2tog, p6; turn. Cont in this way, working 1 less st every WS row until row 15 is worked as foll: P2tog; *do not turn*—1 st rem on RH needle.

Wrong-Side Tier

Wrong-side rectangles

Pick-up row (WS) Pick up and p 8 sts evenly spaced along edge of triangle just worked—9 sts on RH needle; turn.

*Row 1 (RS) K9, turn.

Row 2 P8, p2tog (with last st of rectangle and first st of next triangle, or rectangle); turn. Rep rows 1 and 2 eight times more, *do not turn* at end of last row—one wrong-side rectangle completed.

Next row (WS) Pick up and p 9 sts evenly spaced along edge of next right-side rectangle, turn. Rep from * twice more—3 wrong-side rectangles completed. Turn. [Work a right-side tier followed by a wrong-side tier] 4 times more.

Leaf-Pattern Tier

Work a right-hand corner triangle.

Right-side rectangles

*Pick-up row (RS) Pick up and p 9 sts evenly spaced along edge of next rectangle; turn.

Row 1 (WS) K9; turn.

Row 2 P4, yo, k1, yo, p3, p2tog (with last st of rectangle and first st of next triangle/rectangle); turn.

Row 3 K4, p3, k4; turn.

Row 4 P4, k1, yo, k1, yo, k1, p3, p2tog; turn.

Row 5 K4, p5, k4; turn.

Row 6 P4, k2, yo, k1, yo, k2, p3, p2tog; turn.

Row 7 K4, p7, k4; turn.

Row 8 P4, k3, yo, k1, yo, k3, p3, p2tog; turn.

Row 9 K4, p9, k4; turn.

Row 10 P4, ssk, k5, k2tog, p3, p2tog; turn.

Row 11 K4, p7, k4; turn.

Row 12 P4, ssk, k3, k2tog, p3, p2tog; turn.

Row 13 K4, p5, k4; turn.

Row 14 P4, ssk, k1, k2tog, p3, p2tog; turn.

Row 15 K4, p3, k4; turn.

Row 16 P4, sl 1, k2tog, psso, p3, p2tog; turn.

Row 17 K9, turn.

Row 18 P8, p2tog; *do not turn*. Rep from * across row—2 right-side rectangles completed. Work a left-hand corner triangle.

End triangles

*Pick-up row (WS) Pick up and p 8 sts evenly spaced along edge of triangle just worked—9 sts on RH needle. Turn.

Row 1 (RS) K9; turn.

Row 2 P2tog, p6, p2tog; turn.

Row 3 K8; turn.

Row 4 P2tog, p5, p2tog; turn.

Row 5 K7; turn. Cont to work in this way, working 1 less st between decs until row 16 is worked as foll: P2tog, p2tog, pass first st over 2nd st—1 st rem on RH needle. Rep from * across twice more, picking up sts along edge of rectangles instead of triangle. Fasten off last st.

Finishing

With RS tog, fold bottom edge up, so cast-on edge is just below leaf-pattern tier. Sew side seams. Turn right side out.

I-cord trim

With dpns, cast on 3 sts, leaving a 6"/15cm tail. Work in I-cord as foll: ***Next row (RS)** With 2nd dpn, k3, *do not turn*. Slide sts back to beg of needle to work next row from RS; rep from * for 11"/28cm.

Next row K2tog, k1, pass 2nd st over first st—1 st. Cut yarn, leaving a 6"/15cm tail. Fasten off last st; weave in end. Weave in tail at opposite end. Pin first 4"/10cm of I-cord to straight edge of flap so end of I-cord is even with side edge of flap. Pin last 4"/10cm of I-cord to edge of flap so end of I-cord is even with side edge of flap and a button loop forms in the center of flap. Using a double strand of sewing thread, sew each end of I-cord to edge of flap. Sew on button. ∎

Tulip Scarf

Tulip Scarf

This shapely wraparound necklette will certainly turn heads. The lace edging adds the perfect delicate touch.

Designed by Angela Tong

Skill Level: ■■■□

Materials
- 2 1¾oz/50g skeins (each approx 110 yd/100m) of Noro *Silk Garden* (silk/kid mohair/lamb's wool) in #279 brown/blue/rose
- One pair each size 8 and 10 (5 and 6mm) needles OR SIZE TO OBTAIN GAUGE
- Three size 8 (5mm) double-pointed needles (dpns)

Size
Instructions are written for one size.

Knitted Measurements
Approx 5¼" x 36½"/13.5cm x 92.5cm

Gauge
18 sts and 30 rows to 4"/10cm over garter st using smaller needles. TAKE TIME TO CHECK GAUGE.

Tulip Lace
(over 21 sts)
Row 1 (WS) Purl.
Row 2 K1, [yo, k3, SK2P, k3, yo, k1] twice.
Row 3 Purl.
Row 4 P1, [k1, yo, k2, SK2P, k2, yo, k1, p1] twice.
Row 5 K1, [p9, k1] twice.
Row 6 P1, [k2, yo, k1, SK2P, k1, yo, k2, p1] twice.
Row 7 K1, [p9, k1] twice.
Row 8 P1, [k3, yo, SK2P, yo, k3, p1] twice.
Work rows 1–8 for tulip lace.

Scarf
With smaller needles, cast on 3 sts.
Next (inc) row K1, yo, knit to end—4 sts. Rep this row 20 times more—24 sts. Cont in garter st (knit every row) for 18 rows, end with a WS row.
*Making slot
Divide sts onto 2 dpns as foll: Slip first st on LH needle to first dpn (front dpn), slip next st on LH needle to 2nd dpn (back dpn); cont to alternate sts as established—12 sts on each dpn. Working sts on front dpn, use 3rd dpn to work in k1, p1 rib for 3½"/9cm, end with a WS row. Cut yarn. Join yarn to back dpn and work in k1, p1 rib for 3½"/9cm, end with a WS row. *Do not cut yarn.*
Joining slot
Next row (RS) Holding front dpn in front and back dpn behind, transfer sts to 3rd dpn as foll: Slip first st on front dpn to 3rd dpn, slip first st on back dpn to 3rd dpn, then cont to alternate sts as established to end—24 sts. Change back to smaller needles.* Cont in garter st until piece measures 25"/63.5cm from beg, end with a WS row. Rep from * to * for 2nd slot. Cont in garter st for 18 rows.
Next (dec) row K2tog, yo, k2tog, knit to end—23 sts. Rep this row 20 times more—3 sts. Bind off knitwise.

Lace edging
With RS facing, 3-st cast-on edge at top and larger needles, beg at right corner of shaped edge, then using eyelets, pick up and k 21 sts to left corner. Work rows 1–8 of tulip lace. Bind off sts loosely knitwise. Rep at opposite end of scarf.

Finishing
Wet-block scarf, pinning tulip lace points to create tulip shape. ■

Welted Hat

Welted Hat

Warm, snug and sporty, and knit in a lovely pastel palette, this soft topper will brighten the deepest, darkest February day.

Designed by Jacqueline van Dillen

Skill Level: ■■□□

Materials

- 2 3½oz/100g hanks (each approx 176 yd/161m) of Noro *Kochoran* (wool/silk/angora) in #53 lime/orange/aqua/beige
- One pair size 8 (5mm) needles OR SIZE TO OBTAIN GAUGE

Size

Instructions are written for one size.

Knitted Measurements

Head circumference 21"/53.5cm
Depth 10½"/26.5cm

Gauge

18 sts to 5"/12.5cm and 32 rows to 4"/10cm over welted pat using size 8 (5mm) needles. TAKE TIME TO CHECK GAUGE.

Hat

Cast on 78 sts. Cont in welted pat as foll:
Row 1 (RS) Purl.
Row 2 Knit.
Rows 3 and 4 Purl.
Row 5 Knit.
Rows 6 and 7 Purl.
Row (dec) 8 (WS) K19, k2tog, k36, k2tog, k19—76 sts.
Rows 9–13 Rep rows 3–7.
Row (dec) 14 K19, k2tog, k35, k2tog, k18—74 sts.
Rows 15–19 Rep rows 3–7.
Row (dec) 20 K18, k2tog, k34, k2tog, k18—72 sts.
Rows 21–25 Rep rows 3–7.
Row (dec) 26 K18, k2tog, k33, k2tog, k17—70 sts.
Rows 27–31 Rep rows 3–7.
Row (dec) 32 K17, k2tog, k32, k2tog, k17—68 sts.
Rows 33–37 Rep rows 3–7.
Row (dec) 38 K17, k2tog, k31, k2tog, k16—66 sts.
Rows 39–43 Rep rows 3–7.
Row (dec) 44 K16, k2tog, k30, k2tog, k16—64 sts.
Rows 45–49 Rep rows 3–7.
Row (dec) 50 K16, k2tog, k29, k2tog, k15—62 sts.
Rows 51–55 Rep rows 3–7.
Row (dec) 56 K15, k2tog, k28, k2tog, k15—60 sts.
Rows 57–61 Rep rows 3–7.
Row (dec) 62 K15, k2tog, k27, k2tog, k14—58 sts.
Rows 63–67 Rep rows 3–7.
Row (dec) 68 K14, k2tog, k26, k2tog, k14—56 sts.
Rows 69–73 Rep rows 3–7.
Row (dec) 74 K14, k2tog, k25, k2tog, k13—54 sts.
Rows 75–78 Rep rows 3–6.
Rows 79–84 Rep rows 1–6. Bind off knitwise.

Finishing

Sew long seam (this is now the back seam). With RS together, center back seam over front, then sew top seam. Turn RS out. ■

Modular Neck Wrap

Modular Neck Wrap

Although it takes its inspiration from menswear, this neat, buttoned cowl is decidedly feminine.

Designed by Ginger Luters

Skill Level: ■■■□

Materials

- 2 1¾oz/50g skeins (each approx 110 yd/100m) of Noro *Silk Garden* (silk/kid mohair/lamb's wool) in #282 purple/gold/green
- One pair size 6 (4mm) needles OR SIZE TO OBTAIN GAUGE
- Three ¾"/19mm buttons

Size

Instructions are written for one size

Knitted Measurements

Approx 4½" x 31"/11.5cm x 79cm

Gauge

20 sts and 38 rows to 4"/10cm over garter st (knit every row) using size 6 (4mm) needles. TAKE TIME TO CHECK GAUGE.

Note

Refer to diagram for direction of picked-up sts.

Stitch Glossary

kf&b Inc 1 by knitting into the front and back of the next st.

Neck Wrap

Triangle A

Make a slip knot and place on needle (first st).
Row 1 (RS) In slip knot, work kf&b—2 sts.
Row 2 Knit.
Row 3 K1, kf&b—3 sts.
Row 4 Knit.
Row 5 K1, kf&b, sl 1 wyif; turn—4 sts.
Row 6 K1 tbl, k3.
Row 7 K1, kf&b, k1, sl 1 wyif; turn—5 sts.
Row 8 K1 tbl, k4.
Row 9 K1, kf&b, knit to last st, sl 1 wyif; turn—6 sts.
Row 10 K1 tbl, knit to end.
Rows 11–32 Rep rows 9 and 10 eleven times—17 sts.
Row 33 (RS) K1, ssk, knit to last st, sl 1 wyif; turn—16 sts.
Row 34 K1 tbl, knit to end.
Rows 35–60 Rep rows 31 and 32 thirteen times—3 sts.
Row 61 (RS) K1, ssk—2 sts.
Row 62 Knit.
Row 63 Ssk—1 st.
Row 64 Knit. *Do not cut yarn.* The st rem on needle counts as first st of triangle B.

Triangle B

Row 1 (RS) With RS facing, pick up and k 32 sts along long edge of triangle A—33 sts.
Row 2 Knit to last st, sl 1 wyif; turn.
Row 3 K1 tbl, knit to last 3 sts, k2tog, k1—32 sts.
Row 4 Knit to last st, sl 1 wyif; turn.

Rows 5–62 Rep rows 3 and 4 twenty-nine times—3 sts.

Row 63 K2tog, k1—2 sts.

Row 64 Knit.

Row 65 K2tog—1 st. Cut yarn and fasten off last st.

Triangle C

Row 1 (RS) With RS facing, pick up and k 33 sts along long edge of triangle B.

Row 2 K1 tbl, knit to end.

Row 3 K1, ssk, knit to last st, sl 1 wyif; turn—32 sts.

Row 4 K1 tbl, knit to end.

Rows 5–62 Rep rows 3 and 4 twenty-nine times—3 sts.

Row 63 K1, ssk—2 sts.

Row 64 Knit.

Row 65 Ssk—1 st. *Do not cut yarn.* The st rem on needle counts as first st of triangle D.

Triangle D

Row 1 (RS) With RS facing, pick up and k 32 sts along long edge of triangle C—33 sts. Rep rows 2–65 of triangle B.

Triangle E

Row 1 (RS) With RS facing, pick up and k 33 sts along long edge of triangle D. Rep rows 2–65 of triangle C. *Do not cut yarn.* The st rem on needle counts as first st of triangle F.

Triangle F

Row 1 (RS) With RS facing, pick up and k 32 sts along long edge of triangle E—33 sts. Rep rows 2–65 of triangle B.

Triangle G

Row 1 (RS) With RS facing, pick up and k 33 sts along long edge of triangle F.

Row 2 Knit.

Row 3 K1, ssk, knit to last 3 sts, k2tog, k1—31 sts.

Row 4 Knit.

Rows 5–30 Rep rows 3 and 4 thirteen times—5 sts.

Row 31 Ssk, k1, k2tog—3 sts.

Row 32 Knit.

Row 33 S2KP—1 st. Cut yarn and fasten off last st.

Finishing

Block piece lightly to measurements.

Assembling

Refer to photo. With RS of neck wrap facing, bring triangle G around and place on top triangles A/B, so top edge of G is flush with side edge of A/C, and bottom edge of wrap extends 2"/5cm below side edge of G. Tack edges to secure on WS. Sew on buttons, as shown, working through both layers. ∎

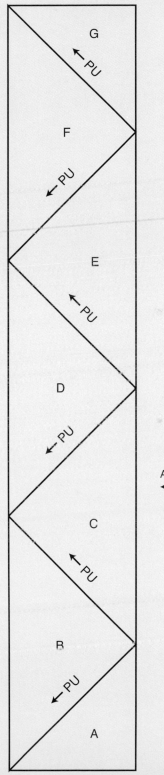

Abbreviation
← PU Pick up following
     direction of arrow

Scale-Pattern Mitts

Scale-Pattern Mitts

Knit in vibrant Impressionist hues, these playful wristers provide a welcome burst of springtime color to brighten winter's grays.

Designed by Amy Polcyn

Skill Level: ■■■□

Materials

- 1 3½oz/100g skein (approx 218 yd/200m) of Noro *Taiyo* (cotton/silk/wool/nylon) in #14 blue/green/hot pink/purple
- One set (5) size 7 (4.5mm) double-pointed needles (dpns) OR SIZE TO OBTAIN GAUGE
- Stitch markers
- Contrasting yarn (waste yarn)

Size

Instructions are written for one size.

Knitted Measurements

Hand circumference 7½"/19cm
Length of cuff approx 3"/7.5cm

Gauge

21 sts and 30 rnds to 4"/10cm over pat st using size 7 (4.5mm) dpns.
TAKE TIME TO CHECK GAUGE.

Stitch Glossary

LS (lifted strand) Insert RH needle (from *front* to *back*) under horizontal strand between last st worked on RH needle and next st on LH needle. Lift strand and leave on RH needle.
kf&b Inc 1 by knitting into the front and back of the next st.

Twisted Rib

(over an even number of sts)
Rnd 1 *K1 tbl, p1; rep from * around.
Rep rnd 1 for twisted rib.

Pattern Stitch (over a multiple of 4 sts)

Rnd 1 Knit.
Rnd 2 *LS, k2, with LH needle, pass LS over these 2 sts, k2; rep from * around.
Rnd 3 Knit.
Rnd 4 *K2, LS, k2, with LH needle, pass LS over these 2 sts; rep from * around.
Rep rnds 1–4 for pat st.

Mitt (make 2)

Cuff

Cast on 40 sts. Divide sts over 4 needles. Join and pm, taking care not to twist sts on needles. Work in twisted rib for 3"/7.5cm. Cont in pat st and work rnds 1 and 2.

Thumb gusset

Inc rnd 1 Work rnd 3 of pat st over first 20 sts, pm, M1, pm, work rnd 3 of pat st over last 20 sts—41 sts (1 st between gusset markers).

Next rnd Work rnd 4 of pat st to marker, sl marker, k1, sl marker, work in pat st to end.

Inc rnd 2 Work rnd 1 of pat st to marker, sl marker, M1, kf&b, M1, sl marker, work in pat st to end—44 sts (4 sts between gusset markers). Work rnds 2–4 of pat st over 4 sts between gusset markers and rem sts.

Inc rnd 3 Work rnd 1 of pat st to marker, sl marker, M1, k4, M1, sl marker, work in pat st to end—46 sts (6 sts between gusset markers). Work rnds 2–4 of pat st over 6 sts between gusset markers (working new sts into pat st as sts become available), work rnds 2–4 over rem sts as established.

Inc rnd 4 Work rnd 1 of pat st to marker, sl marker, M1, k6, M1, sl marker, work in pat st to end—48 sts (8 sts between gusset markers). Work rnd 2 of pat st over 8 sts between gusset markers (working new sts into pat st as sts become available), work rnd 2 over rem sts as established.

Inc rnd 5 Work rnd 3 of pat st to marker, sl marker, M1, k8, M1, sl marker, work in pat st to end—50 sts (10 sts between gusset markers). Work rnd 4 of pat st over 10 sts between gusset markers (working new sts into pat st as sts become available), work rnd 4 over rem sts as established.

Inc rnd 6 Work rnd 1 of pat st to marker, sl marker, M1, k10, M1, sl marker, work in pat st to end—52 sts (12 sts between gusset markers). Work rnd 2 of pat st over 12 sts between gusset markers (working new sts into pat st as sts become available), work rnd 2 over rem sts as established.

Inc rnd 7 Work rnd 3 of pat st to marker, sl marker, M1, k12, M1, sl marker, work in pat st to end—54 sts (14 sts between gusset markers).

Next rnd Work rnd 4 of pat st to marker, place next 14 sts on waste yarn for thumb (dropping markers), work to end of rnd—40 sts.

Hand

Cont in pat st as established until piece measures 7"/18cm from beg. Work in twisted rib for 1"/2.5cm. Bind off in twisted rib.

Thumb

Place 14 thumb gusset sts over 3 needles.

Next rnd Join yarn at inside of thumb, then work in twisted rib across 14 sts. Join and pm for beg of rnds. Cont in rib for 4 rnds more. Bind off in twisted rib. ∎

Slip-Stitch Cowl

Slip-Stitch Cowl

Romantic and lush, but so practical, this infinity scarf will be your go-everywhere wrap, from a night at the opera to a trip to the corner market.

Designed by Valerie Zumwalt

Skill Level: ■■■□

Materials

■ 2 1¾oz/50g skeins (each approx 110 yd/100m) of Noro *Kureyon* (wool) each in #255 brown/red/gold (A) and #242 rust/olive/black (B)
■ Size 8 (5mm) circular needle, 24"/61cm long, OR SIZE TO OBTAIN GAUGE
■ Stitch marker

Size

Instructions are written for one size.

Knitted Measurements

Circumference approx 46"/117cm
Length approx 10"/25.5cm

Gauge

19 sts and 36 rnds to 4"/10cm over slip st pat using size 8 (5mm) circular needle. TAKE TIME TO CHECK GAUGE.

Cowl

With A, cast on 221 sts. Join and pm taking care not to twist sts on needle.
Set-up rnds
Rnds 1–3 With A, k1, *p3, k3; rep from * around to last 4 sts, end p3, k1.
Cont in slip st pat as foll:
Rnd 1 With A, k1, *p3, k3; rep from * around to last 4 sts, end p3, k1.
Rnd 2 With B, k1, *k3, sl 3 wyib; rep from * around to last 4 sts, end k4.
Rnd 3 With B, k1, *k4, sl 1 wyib, k1; rep from * around to last 4 sts, end k4.
Rnd 4 With B, knit.
Rnd 5 With B, k1, *k3, p3; rep from * around to last 4 sts, end k4.
Rnd 6 With A, k1, *sl 3 wyib, k3; rep from * around to last 4 sts, end sl 3 wyib, k1.
Rnd 7 With A, k1, *k1, sl 1 wyib, k4; rep from * around to last 4 sts, end k1, sl 1 wyib, k2.
Rnd 8 With A, knit. Rep rnds 1–8 nine times more, then rnds 1–4 once.
Last 3 rnds With B, k1, *k3, p3; rep from * around to last 4 sts, end k4. Bind off loosely knitwise.

Finishing

Block piece lightly to measurements. ■

Lacy Pillows

Zigzag
Pillow

Leaves and Cables
Pillow

Diamond-Wave
Pillow

Leaves and Cables Pillow

Alternating muted and brighter tones create the perfect background for a subtle cable pattern.

Designed by Therese Chynoweth

Skill Level: ■■■□

Materials

- 4 1¾oz/50g skeins (each approx 110 yd/100m) of Noro *Silk Garden* (silk/kid mohair/lamb's wool) in #323 rust/brown/pink/blue
- One pair size 7 (4.5mm) needles OR SIZE TO OBTAIN GAUGE
- Cable needle (cn)
- Two 17" x 17"/43cm x 43cm squares of medium-weight cotton fabric (to cover pillow form)
- 16"/41cm square knife-edge pillow form
- Six 1"/25mm buttons
- Six large metal snaps
- Matching sewing thread
- Sewing needle
- Sewing machine

Size

Instructions are written for one size.

Knitted Measurements

Approx 16" x 16"/40.5cm x 40.5cm

Gauge

22 sts and 24 rows to 4"/10cm over chart pat using size 7 (4.5mm) needles (after blocking). TAKE TIME TO CHECK GAUGE.

Stitch Glossary

4-st RC Sl 2 sts to cn and hold to *back*, k2, k2 from cn.
4-st LC Sl 2 sts to cn and hold to *front*, k2, k2 from cn.

Pillow Cover

Cast on 86 sts.
Top border
Rows 1 and 3 K2, *p2, k2; rep from * to end.
Rows 2 and 4 P2, *k2, p2; rep from* to end.
Beg chart pat
Row 1 Work 26-st rep 3 times, then work last 8 sts. Cont to foll chart in this way to row 20, then rep rows 1–20 until piece measures approx 31"/78.5cm from beg, end with row 10 or 20.
Bottom border
Rep rows 2–4 of top border, then row 1. Bind off in rib.

Finishing

Block piece lightly.
Covering pillow form
Place fabric squares together, right sides facing. Machine-stitch pieces together using a ½"/1.3cm seam allowance and leaving an 8"/20.5cm opening in center bottom. Clip corners. Turn RS out; press. Insert pillow form. Slip stitch opening closed.
Assembling pillow cover
Place pillow cover RS up on work surface, so top (cast-on) edge is at top. Fold down top edge 5½"/14cm; pin side edges. Fold up bottom edge so bottom border overlaps top border by ¾"/2cm; pin side edges and across borders. Sew side seams; remove pins. Turn RS out. Place markers for 6 buttons along top border, with the first and last 2"/5cm from side seams and the others evenly spaced between. Using a double strand of sewing thread, sew on buttons. On WS of top border, sew bottom halves of metal snaps behind buttons. Sew top halves of snaps to bottom border. Insert covered pillow form into pillow cover. Snap opening closed. ■
(Chart on page 136)

Zigzag Pillow

Lacy eyelets play peekaboo in this textured zigzag pattern.

Designed by Therese Chynoweth

Skill Level: ■■■□

Materials
- 4 1¾oz/50g skeins (each approx 110 yd/100m) of Noro *Silk Garden* (silk/kid mohair/lamb's wool) in #323 rust/brown/pink/blue
- Two size 7 (4.5mm) circular needles, 24"/60cm long OR SIZE TO OBTAIN GAUGE
- Spare size 7 (4.5mm) needle (for 3-needle bind-off)
- Stitch markers
- Two 17" x 17"/43cm x 43cm squares of medium-weight cotton fabric (to cover pillow form)
- 16"/41cm square knife-edge pillow form
- Matching sewing thread
- Sewing needle
- Sewing machine

Size
Instructions are written for one size.

Knitted Measurements
Approx 16" x 16"/40.5cm x 40.5cm

Gauge
17 sts and 20 rnds to 4"/10cm over chart pat using size 7 (4.5mm) circular needle (after blocking). TAKE TIME TO CHECK GAUGE.

Note
To work in the rnd, always read chart from right to left.

Pillow Cover
With circular needle, cast on 67 sts, pm, cast on 67 sts more—134 sts. Join taking care not to twist sts on needle, pm for beg of rnds.
Bottom border
Rnds 1 and 3 Knit.
Rnds 2 and 4 Purl.
Beg chart pat
Rnd 1 *Work first st, work 10-st rep 6 times, work last 6 sts; rep from * once more. Cont to foll chart in this way to rnd 12, then rep rnds 1–12 until piece measures approx 15"/38cm from beg, end with an even rnd.
Top border
Rep rnds 1–4 of bottom border. Place first 67 sts on 2nd circular needle, leaving rem 67 sts on first needle. Turn piece WS out. Join front and back tog using 3-needle bind-off. Turn piece RS out.

Finishing
Block piece lightly.
Covering pillow form
Place fabric squares together, right sides facing. Machine-stitch pieces together using a ½"/1.3cm seam allowance and leaving an 8"/20.5cm opening in center bottom. Clip corners. Turn RS out; press. Insert pillow form. Slip stitch opening closed. Insert covered pillow form into pillow cover. Sew opening closed. ∎

(Chart on page 137)

Diamond-Wave Pillow

An undulating wave pattern creates a relaxing vibe for this comfy pillow.

Designed by Therese Chynoweth

Skill Level: ■■■□

Materials

- 4 1¾oz/50g skeins (each approx 110 yd/100m) of Noro *Silk Garden* (silk/kid mohair/lamb's wool) in #323 rust/brown/pink/blue
- Two size 7 (4.5mm) circular needles, 24"/60cm long OR SIZE TO OBTAIN GAUGE
- Spare size 7 (4.5mm) needle (for 3-needle bind-off)
- Stitch markers
- Cable needle (cn)
- 16"/41cm square knife-edge pillow form

Size

Instructions are written for one size.

Knitted Measurements

Approx 16" x 16"/40.5cm x 40.5cm

Gauge

21 sts and 24 rnds to 4"/10cm over chart pat using size 7 (4.5mm) circular needle (unstretched). TAKE TIME TO CHECK GAUGE.

Note

To work in the rnd, always read chart from right to left.

Stitch Glossary

4-st RC Sl 2 sts to cn and hold to *back*, k2 k2 from cn.
4-st LC Sl 2 sts to cn and hold to *front*, k2, k2 from cn.
M1 p-st (make 1 purl stitch) Insert LH needle from *front* to *back* under the strand between the last st worked and the next st. Purl strand through back loop to twist the st.

Pillow Cover

With circular needle, cast on 160 sts. Join, taking care not to twist sts on needle, pm for beg of rnds.
Bottom border
Work in k1, p1 rib for ¾"/2cm.
Beg chart pat
Rnd 1 Work 16-st rep 10 times. Cont to foll chart in this way to rnd 32, then rep rnds 1–32 once more, then rnds 1–20 once. Piece should measure approx 14¾"/37.5cm from beg.
Top border
Work in k1, p1 rib for ¾"/2cm. Place first 80 sts on 2nd circular needle, leaving rem 80 sts on first needle. Turn piece WS out. Join front and back tog using 3-needle bind-off. Turn piece RS out.

Finishing

Block piece lightly. Insert pillow form. Sew opening closed. ■
(Chart on page 137)

Braided Headband

Braided Headband

You'll keep your ears toasty warm while making a bold fashion statement when you wear this stunning waffle-stitch headpiece.

Designed by Lynn M. Wilson

Skill Level: ■■■☐

Materials

- 2 1¾oz/50g skeins (each approx 110 yd/100m) of Noro *Silk Garden* (silk/kid mohair/lamb's wool) in #279 brown/blue/rose/purple
- Contrasting worsted-weight yarn (waste yarn)
- One pair size 7 (4.5mm) needles OR SIZE TO OBTAIN GAUGE
- Three size 7 (4.5mm) double-pointed needles (dpns)
- Size H/8 (5mm) crochet hook (for chain-stitch provisional cast-on)
- Stitch holders
- Safety pins
- One 1¼"/31mm button
- Matching sewing thread (optional)

Size

Instructions are written for one size.

Knitted Measurements

Head circumference 21"/53.5cm (unstretched)
Width approx 4½"/11.5cm

Gauge

22 sts and 34 rows to 4"/10cm over waffle st using size 7 (4.5mm) needles. TAKE TIME TO CHECK GAUGE.

Stitch Glossary

kf&b Inc 1 by knitting into the front and back of the next st.

Waffle Stitch

(over a multiple of 3 sts plus 1)
Note Sl all sts purlwise.
Row 1 (RS) K3, *k1 wrapping yarn twice around needle, k2; rep from * to last st, end k1.
Row 2 K1, *p2, sl 1 wyif, dropping extra wrap from needle; rep from * to last 3 sts, end p2, k1.
Row 3 K3, *sl 1 wyif, k2; rep from * to last st, end k1.
Row 4 K3, *sl 1 wyif, k2; rep from * to last st, end k1.
Rep rows 1–4 for waffle st.

Headband

Strip A
With crochet hook and waste yarn, ch 16 for chain-st provisional cast-on. Cut yarn and draw end though lp on hook. Turn ch so bottom lps are at top and cut end is at left. With straight needles, beg 2 lps from right end, pick up and k 1 st in each of next 11 lps—11 sts. Knit next 2 rows.
Next (inc) row (RS) K1, kf&b, k7, kf&b, k1—13 sts. Knit next row. Cont in waffle st and work even until piece measures 20"/51cm from beg, end with row 4. Knit next row.
Next (dec) row (WS) K1, k2tog, k7, k2tog, k1—11 sts. Cut yarn. Place sts on a dpn. Lightly steam-block strip.
Strip B
Work same as strip A.
Strip C
Work same as strip A. *Do not cut yarn.*
Joining strip A to strip B

Next (joining) row (RS) With RS facing, place strip A behind strip C and so dpns are parallel, *insert 3rd dpn knitwise into first st of each needle and wrap yarn around each needle as if to knit, then knit these 2 sts tog and sl them off the needles; rep from * to end—11 sts. Knit next row. Leave sts on needle.

Joining strip A/C to strip B

Next (joining) row (RS) With RS facing, place strip B behind strip A/C and so dpns are parallel, *insert 3rd dpn knitwise into first st of each needle and wrap yarn around each needle as if to knit, then knit these 2 sts tog and sl them off the needles; rep from * to end—11 sts. Knit next row. Leave sts on needle.

Buttonband

Cont in garter st (knit every row) until piece measures 2½"/6.5cm from last joining.

Next (dec) row K1, k2tog, k5, k2tog, k1—9 sts.

Next (dec) row K1, k2tog, k3, k2tog, k1—7 sts.

Next (dec) row K1, k2tog, k1, k2tog, k1—5 sts. Bind off knitwise.

Preparing strips for braiding

With RS facing and working one strip at a time, release cut end from lp of waste yarn ch. Pulling out 1 ch at a time, place 11 live sts on holder.

Braiding strips

Loosely braid strips. Use safety pins to secure braid. Place sts from each holder onto a dpn.

Joining strips

Next (joining) row (RS) With RS facing, join top strip and strip behind it same as joining strip A/C to strip B.

Next (joining) row (RS) With RS facing, join first two strips to last strip same as joining strip A/C to strip B.

Buttonhole band

Cont in garter st (knit every row) until piece measures 2¼"/5.5cm from last joining.

Next (dec) row K1, k2tog, k5, k2tog, k1—9 sts.

Next (dec) row K1, k2tog, k3, k2tog, k1—7 sts.

Next (dec) row K1, k2tog, k1, k2tog, k1—5 sts.

Next (buttonhole) row K1, k2tog, yo twice, k2.

Next row K2, knit into front and back of double yo, k2—6 sts. Bind off loosely knitwise.

Finishing

To hold braid in place, tack strips tog on WS using sewing thread or yarn. Sew on button. ∎

Welted Cowl

Welted Cowl

Two dazzling colorways plus a bold stitch pattern equal a gorgeous accessory that will wrap you in style.

Designed by Erica Schlueter

Skill Level: ■■□□

Materials
- 2 3½oz/100g hanks (each approx 131 yd/120m) of Noro *Iro* (wool/silk) each in #94 brown/green/grey (A) and #95 blue/green/bronze (B)
- Size 11 (8mm) circular needle, 24"/61cm long OR SIZE TO OBTAIN GAUGE
- Stitch marker

Size
Instructions are written for one size.

Knitted Measurements
Circumference (around bottom) approx 32"/81cm
Circumference (around top) approx 27"/68.5cm
Length approx 18½"/47cm

Gauge
11 sts and 18 rnds to 4"/10cm over welted stripe pat using size 11 (8mm) circular needle. TAKE TIME TO CHECK GAUGE.

Welted Stripe Pattern
Rnds 1–3 With A, purl.
Rnds 4–7 With B, knit.
Rnd 8 With A, knit.
Rep rnds 1–8 for welted stripe pat.

Cowl
With A, cast on 88 sts. Join and pm, taking care not to twist sts on needle. Work even in welted stripe pat for 8 rnds. Cont in welted stripe pat, dec 1 st at end of next rnd (p2tog on purl rnds and k2tog on knit rnds), then every 5th rnd 13 times more—74 sts. Work even until 11 B stripes have been completed, end with rnd 7.
Next rnd With A, knit.
Next 2 rnds With A, purl. Bind off loosely purlwise.

Finishing
Block piece lightly to measurements. ■

Riverbed Rib Hat

Riverbed Rib Hat

Knit in shades of purple and mossy greens, the flowing ribs of this pretty cap echo the rippling waters of a stream.

Designed by Katherine Vaughan

Skill Level: ■■■□

Materials

- 1 3½oz/100g hank (approx 131 yd/120m) of Noro *Iro* (wool/silk) in #106 green/teal/purple/lilac
- Sizes 9 and 10 (5.5 and 6mm) circular needles, 16"/40cm long, OR SIZE TO OBTAIN GAUGE
- One set (5) size 10 (6mm) double-pointed needles (dpns)
- Stitch marker

Size

Instructions are written for one size.

Knitted Measurements

Head circumference 19"/48cm (unstretched)
Depth 9"/23cm

Gauge

13 sts and 22 rnds to 4"/10cm over riverbed rib using size 10 (6mm) circular needle. TAKE TIME TO CHECK GAUGE.

Riverbed Rib

(over a multiple of 9 sts)
Rnds 1–6 *K1, p2, k3, p2, k1; rep from * around.
Rnd 7 *K1, p2, k1, drop next st, k1, p2, k1, yo; rep from * around.
Rnds 8–13 *K1, [p2, k2] twice; rep from * around.
Rnd 14 *K1, p2, k1, yo, k1, p2, k1, drop next st; rep from * around.
Rep rnds 1–14 for riverbed rib.

Hat

With smaller circular needle, cast on 56 sts. Join and pm taking care not to twist sts on needle. Work in k2, p2 rib as foll:
Next rnd *K1, p2, k1; rep from * around. Rep this rnd for 1"/2.5cm. Change to larger circular needle.
Next (set-up) rnd *K1, p2, k1, yo, k1, p2, k1; rep from * around—63 sts. Work rnds 1–14 of riverbed rib once, then rnds 1–13 once.

Crown shaping

Change to dpns (dividing sts evenly between 4 needles) when there are too few sts on circular needle.
Dec rnd 1 *K1, p2tog, k1, yo, k1, p2tog, k1, drop next st; rep from * around—49 sts.
Next 4 rnds *K1, p1, k3, p1, k1; rep from * around.
Dec rnd 2 *P2tog, k3, p2tog; rep from * around—35 sts.
Next 2 rnds *P1, k3, p1; rep from * around.
Dec rnd 3 *P1, k1, drop next st, k1, p1; rep from * around—28 sts.
Dec rnd 4 *K2tog, ssk; rep from * around—14 sts.
Next rnd Knit.
Dec rnd 5 [K2tog] 7 times—7 sts. Cut yarn leaving an 8"/20.5cm tail and thread through rem sts. Pull tog tightly and secure end. ■

Kimono Shrug

Kimono Shrug
Graceful parasol-stitch sleeves add flair to this shrug knit side to side in bright shades of purple and pink.

Designed by Edna Hart

Skill Level: ■■■□

Materials
- 7 1¾oz/50g skeins (each approx 110 yd/100m) of Noro *Kureyon* (wool) in #250 purple/red/royal
- One pair size 8 (5mm) needles OR SIZE TO OBTAIN GAUGE

Sizes
Instructions are written for X-Small/Small. Changes for Medium/Large and 1X/2X are in parentheses.

Knitted Measurements
Across back 19 (23, 27)"/48 (58.5, 68.5)cm
Upper arm 22"/56cm

Gauge
16 sts and 24 rows to 4"/10cm over pat sts using size 8 (5mm) needles. TAKE TIME TO CHECK GAUGE.

Faggoting Rib
(over a multiple of 4 sts)
Row 1 (RS) K4, *yo, SKP, k2; rep from * to end.
Row 2 P4, *yo, p2tog, p2; rep from * to end.
Rep rows 1 and 2 for faggoting rib.

Parasol Stitch
(over a multiple of 18 sts plus 1)
Row 1 (RS) K1, *yo, k1, [p3, k1] 4 times, yo, k1; rep from * to end.
Row 2 and all WS rows Purl.
Row 3 K1,*k1, yo, k1, [p3, k1] 4 times, yo, k2; rep from * to end.
Row 5 K1,*k2, yo, k1, [p3, k1] 4 times, yo, k3; rep from * to end.
Row 7 K1,*k3, yo, k1, [p2tog, p1, k1] 4 times, yo, k4; rep from * to end.
Row 9 K1,*k4, yo, k1, [p2tog, k1] 4 times, yo, k5; rep from * to end.
Row 11 K1,*k5, yo, k1, [p3tog, k1] twice, yo, k6; rep from * to end.
Row 12 Purl.
Rep rows 1–12 for parasol st.

Body
Cast on 92 sts. Work even in faggoting rib until piece measures 24 (28, 32)"/61 (71, 81)cm from beg, end with a WS row. Bind off all sts knitwise.

Sleeves (make 2)
Cast on 91 sts. Cont in parasol st and rep rows 1–12 four times. Bind off knitwise.

Finishing

Sew in sleeves. Block piece to measurements. Sew a 10"/25.5cm underarm seam each side.

Neck edging

Cast on 91 (109, 127) sts. Cont in parasol st, working rows 1–12 once. Bind off knitwise. Block piece. With RS tog, pin bound-off edge of neck edging to top edge of body, easing in fullness evenly across. Sew neck edging in place. Block seam. ■

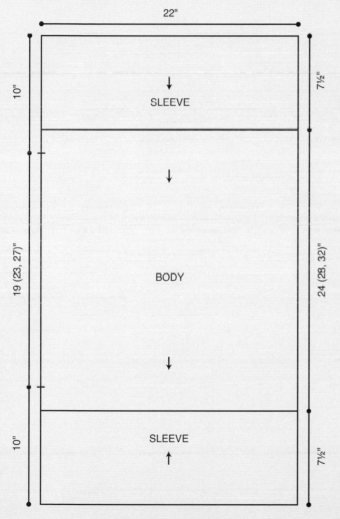

22"

10"

SLEEVE

7½"

19 (23, 27)"

BODY

24 (28, 32)"

10"

SLEEVE

7½"

← Direction of work

Stitch-Sampler Tote

Back

Autumn Sampler Tote

A beautiful harvest of stitch patterns in shades of russet, gold and brown combine to create a carry-all that's perfect for toting library books or apples from the market.

Designed by Cheryl Murray

Skill Level: ■■■□

Materials

- 5 1¾oz/50g skeins (each approx 110 yd/100m) of Noro *Kureyon* (wool) in #255 brown/red/gold
- One pair size 8 (5mm) needles OR SIZE TO OBTAIN GAUGE
- Size H/8 (5mm) crochet hook
- One 1⅝"/41mm button
- ½ yd/.5m of 45"/114.5cm wide fabric (for lining)
- 1 yd/1m heavyweight fusible interfacing
- Sewing thread to match fabric
- Sewing needle
- One pair round braided leather handles, 24"/61cm long in dark brown
- Magnetic purse clasp (optional)

Size

Instructions are written for one size.

Knitted Measurements

Approx 14"/35.5cm wide x 16"/40.5cm high x 4"/10cm deep (before felting; excluding handles)

Gauge

17 sts and 28 rows to 4"/10cm over St st (k on RS, p on WS) using size 8 (5mm) needles (before felting). TAKE TIME TO CHECK GAUGE.

Notes

1) Blocks, sides and bottom are each worked separately.
2) Pieces are joined with slip st crochet before felting.

Stitch Glossary

3-st RPC Sl next st to cn and hold to *back*, k2, p1 from cn.
3-st LPC Sl next 2 sts to cn and hold to *front*, p1, k2 from cn.
4-st RC Sl 2 sts to cn and hold to *back*, k2, k2 from cn.
4-st LC Sl 2 sts to cn and hold to *front*, k2, k2 from cn.
4-st RPC Sl 2 sts to cn and hold to *back*, k2, p2 from cn.
4-st LPC Sl 2 sts to cn and hold to *front*, p2, k2 from cn.
6-st RC Sl 3 sts to cn and hold to *back*, k3, k3 from cn.
6-st LC Sl 3 sts to cn and hold to *front*, k3, k3 from cn.

Front

Each block should measure 7" x 8"/18cm x 20.5cm.

Block A
Cast on 28 sts. Cont in reverse St st as foll:
Row 1 (RS) Purl.
Row 2 Knit. Rep rows 1 and 2 until piece measures 8"/20.5cm from beg, end with a WS row. Bind off.

Block B
Cast on 38 sts. Cont in cable and rib st as foll:
Beg chart pat I
Row 1 (RS) Work first 2 sts, work 12-st rep 3 times. Cont to foll chart in this way to row 6, then rep rows 1–6 for cable pat. Work even until piece measures 8"/20.5cm from beg, end with a WS row. Bind off.

Block C
Cast on 38 sts. Cont in lattice cable as foll:
Beg chart pat II
Row 1 (RS) Work 38 sts of chart. Cont to foll chart in this way to row 12, then rep rows 1–12 for cable pat. Work even until piece measures 8"/20.5cm from beg, end with a WS row. Bind off.

Block D

Cast on 38 sts. Cont in broken rib st as foll:

Rows 1, 3 and 5 (RS) K1, *k2, p2; rep from *, end k1.

Rows 2, 4 and 6 P1, *k2, p2; rep from *, end p1.

Rows 7, 9 and 11 K1, *p2, k2; rep from *, end k1.

Rows 8, 10 and 12 P1, *p2, k2; rep from *, end p1. Rep rows 1–12 until piece measures 8"/20.5cm from beg, end with a WS row. Bind off.

Back

Each block should measure 7" x 8"/18cm x 20.5cm.

Block E

Cast on 28 sts. Cont in moss st as foll:

Row 1 (RS) K2, *p1, k1; rep from * to end.

Row 2 *P1, k1; rep from *, end p2.

Row 3 K1, *p1, k1; rep from *, end k1.

Row 4 P1, *k1, p1; rep from *, end p1. Rep rows 1–4 until piece measures 8"/20.5cm from beg, end with a WS row. Bind off.

Block F

Cast on 38 sts. Cont in saxon braid cable as foll:

Beg chart pat III

Row 1 (WS) Work 38 sts of chart. Cont to foll chart in this way to row 16, then rep rows 1–16 for cable pat. Work even until piece measures 8"/20.5cm from beg, end with a WS row. Bind off.

Block G

Cast on 38 sts. Cont in chevron cable pat as foll:

Beg chart pat IV

Row 1 (RS) Work first st, work 12 st rep 3 times, work last st. Cont to foll chart in this way to row 8, then rep rows 1–8 for cable pat. Work even until piece measures 8"/20.5cm from beg, end with a WS row. Bind off.

Block H

Work same as block A.

Sides (make 2)

Cast on 18 sts. Cont in St st until piece measures 16"/40.5cm from beg. Bind off. Piece should measure 4" x 16"/10cm x 40.5cm.

Bottom

Cast on 60 sts. Cont in St st until piece measures 4"/10cm from beg. Bind off. Piece should measure 14" x 4"/35.5cm x 10cm.

Finishing

Following placement diagram for front, join pieces as foll: With WS of block A and C tog, slip st crochet bottom edge of block A to top edge of block C. With WS of block B and D tog, slip st crochet bottom edge of block B to top edge of block D.

With WS tog, slip st crochet RH side edge of blocks A/C to LH side edge of blocks B/D. Following placement diagram for back, join pieces as foll: With WS of block E and G tog, slip st crochet bottom edge of block E to top edge of block G. With WS of block F and H tog, slip st crochet bottom edge of block F to top edge of block H. With WS tog, slip st crochet RH side edge of blocks E/G to LH side edge of blocks F/H. With WS tog, slip st crochet back and front to sides, then join bottom.

I-cord bind-off edging

With RS facing and circular needle, beg at any top corner and pick up 156 sts around top edge of bag. Using cable cast-on method, cast on 3 sts more to LH needle. I-cord rnd *K2, ssk, slip 3 sts from RH needle back to LH needle; rep from * around until all sts have been worked. Cut yarn leaving a long tail. Use tail to graft ends of I-cord tog.

Felting

Note Bag is designed to be just lightly felted. Avoid over felting to prevent loss of stitch pattern definition and excessive shrinkage. Place assembled bag into a zippered lingerie bag or pillowcase. Set washing machine to hot water, small load cycle. Add a small amount of mild detergent or wool wash. Include an old pair of jeans to increase agitation. Start washer. Stop washer every 5 minutes and check for felting. Once desired degree of felting is achieved, remove bag from washer. Remove bag from lingerie bag or pillowcase, then rinse well in cool water. Roll up bag in a large towel and squeeze to remove excess water. Block bag to measurements over a plastic covered box until dry. Sew button to center front of bag; as shown.

Lining

Cut 2 fabric pieces 1"/2.5cm wider and 1½"/4cm taller than front and back. Cut 2 fabric pieces 1"/2.5cm wider and 1¼"/4cm taller than sides. Cut one fabric piece 1"/2.5cm wider and longer than bottom. Cut 2 interfacing pieces ½"/1.3cm narrower and 1"/2.5cm shorter than front and back linings. Cut 2 interfacing pieces ½"/1.3cm narrower and 1"/2.5cm shorter than side linings. Cut one interfacing piece ½"/1.3cm narrower and shorter than bottom lining. Centering each interfacing piece on WS of lining piece, fuse following manufacturer's instructions. Sew lining pieces tog using a ½"/1.3cm seam allowance. Press seams open. Insert lining into bag. Fold top edge of lining over to WS so folded edge is even with bottom edge of I-cord edging. Remove lining; press fold. Install magnetic purse clasp following manufacturer's instructions. Attach handles following manufacturer's instructions. Insert lining back into bag. Hand-stitch top edge of lining in place. ■ (Charts and diagrams on page 138)

Intarsia Lace Scarf

Intarsia Lace Scarf

A single colorway of *Silk Garden* divided into three balls and knit in vertical intarsia stripes creates a veritable rainbow of color.

Designed by Patty Nance

Skill Level: ■■■□

Materials

- 1 1¾oz/50g skein (approx 110 yd/100m) of Noro *Silk Garden* (silk/kid mohair/lamb's wool) in #301 royal/purple/fuchsia/lime
- One pair size 6 (4mm) needles OR SIZE TO OBTAIN GAUGE
- Three zipper-lock storage bags

Stitch Key

☐	Knit on RS, purl on WS
⊟	Purl on RS, knit on WS
Ⅴ	Sl 1 purlwise
Ⓞ	Yarn over
⊠	K2tog on RS, p2tog on WS
⊠	Ssk on RS, p2tog tbl on WS

Size

Instructions are written for one size.

Knitted Measurements

Approx 7" x 55"/18cm x 140cm

Gauge

22 sts and 26 rows to 4"/10cm over chart pat using size 6 (4mm) needles. TAKE TIME TO CHECK GAUGE.

Notes

1) Divide yarn into three balls, approx 36½ yd/33.5m each.
2) Mark one bag #1, one bag #2 and rem bag #3.
3) Place one ball in each bag. Zip almost closed. Feed tail through opening to knit.
4) When changing colors, pick up new color from under dropped color to prevent holes.

Scarf

With color #3, cast on 14 sts; with color #2, cast on 11 sts; with color #1, cast on 14 sts— 39 sts. Changing colors as established, knit next 2 rows.

Beg Chart Pat

Row 1 (RS) With color #1, work first 3 sts, then work 11-st rep once; with color #2, work 11-st rep once; with color #3, work 11-st rep once, then work last 3 sts. Cont to foll chart in this way to row 20, then rep rows 1–20 seventeen times more. Changing colors as established, knit next 2 rows. Bind off knitwise.

Finishing

Block piece lightly to measurements. ■

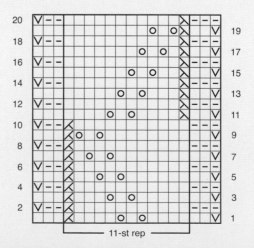

11-st rep

Entrelac Mittens

Entrelac Mittens

The bold blocks of color created by the entrelac technique make the most of this brilliant *Kureyon* colorway.

Designed by Holli Yeoh

Skill Level: ■■■■

Materials

- 2 1¾oz/50g skeins (each approx 110 yd/100m) of Noro *Kureyon* (wool) in #256 pink/orange/teal
- Size 6 (4mm) circular needle, 32"/80cm long, OR SIZE TO OBTAIN GAUGE
- One set (5) each sizes 4 and 6 (3.5 and 4mm) double-pointed needles (dpns)
- Stitch markers
- Locking stitch markers
- Small coilless safety pins

Size

Instructions are written for one size.

Knitted Measurements

Hand circumference 7"/18cm
Length of cuff approx 3"/7.5cm

Gauge

20 sts and 33 rows to 4"/10cm over St st (knit every rnd) using size 6 (4mm) needle. TAKE TIME TO CHECK GAUGE.

Notes

1) Slip all sts purlwise unless otherwise noted. Have yarn in back when slipping sts on RS rows and slip sts with yarn in front on WS rows.
2) Use regular stitch markers unless stated otherwise.
3) To keep track of diamond numbers, attach safety pins to diamonds as they are finished as foll: one safety pin on diamond 1, two safety pins on diamond 2, etc.

Stitch Glossary

ssp (slip, slip, purl) Sl first st knitwise, then sl next st knitwise. Slip these 2 sts back to LH needle, then purl them tog tbl.
kf&b Inc 1 by knitting into the front and back of the next st.
M1R Insert LH needle from back to front into strand between last st worked and next st on LH needle. Knit into front loop to twist the st.
M1L Insert LH needle from front to back into strand between last st worked and next st on LH needle. Knit into back loop to twist the st.

Mittens (make 2)

Cuff

With smaller dpn, cast on 36 sts. Divide sts over 4 needles. Join, taking care not to twist sts on needles, pm for beg of rnds. Work around in k1, p1 rib for 3"/7.5cm. Change to circular needle.
Next (dec) rnd *[K1, k2tog, k1, ssk] 3 times, pull circular needle through sts so they rest far enough along cable and needle is free to work next sts; rep from * once more—24 sts. Remove marker.

Base triangles

Entrelac triangles are worked back and forth in short rows. *Pull needle through so sts rest on cable and needle is free to work next sts.
Row 1 (RS) K1; turn.
Row 2 P1; turn.
Row 3 Sl 1, k1; turn.
Row 4 and all WS rows Sl 1, purl to end; turn.
Row 5 Sl 1, k2; turn.
Row 7 Sl 1, k3; turn.
Row 9 Sl 1, k4; turn. Cont to work one more st every RS row 6 times more. Cont as foll:
Row 23 Sl 1, k11; do not turn—12 sts (one base triangle completed). Rep from * for one more triangle—2 base triangles made.

Diamond 1 with thumb gusset

Don't pull circular needle through sts.

Pick-up row (RS) With RS facing, beg at lower corner of first base triangle, pm, M1, pm, pick up and k 12 sts evenly along right edge of first base triangle; turn.

Row 1 Sl 1, p9, ssp, sl marker, p1, sl marker, p1; turn.

Row 2 Kf&b, sl marker, (M1L, k1, M1R) for thumb gusset, sl marker, k11; turn.

Row 3 and all WS rows to row 19 Sl 1, purl to 2 sts before marker, ssp, sl marker, purl to next marker, sl marker, purl to 1 st before gap, p2tog (last st of diamond 1 and first st of base triangle); turn.

Row 4 Sl 1, M1R, k1, sl marker, M1L, k3, M1R, sl marker, k10; turn.

Row 6 Sl 1, k1, M1R, k1, sl marker, k5, sl marker, k9; turn.

Row 8 Sl 1, k2, M1R, k1, sl marker, M1L, k5, M1R, sl marker, k8; turn.

Row 10 Sl 1, k3, M1R, k1, sl marker, M1L, k7, M1R, sl marker, k7; turn.

Row 12 Sl 1, k4, M1R, k1, sl marker, k9, sl marker, k6; turn.

Row 14 Sl 1, k5, M1R, k1, sl marker, M1L, k9, M1R, sl marker, k5; turn.

Row 16 Sl 1, k6, M1R, k1, sl marker, M1L, k11, M1R, sl marker, k4; turn.

Row 18 Sl 1, k7, M1R, k1, sl marker, k13, sl marker, k3; turn.

Row 20 Sl 1, k8, M1R, k1, sl marker, M1L, k13, M1R, sl marker, k2; turn.

Row 21 Ssp, sl marker, p15, p10, sl marker, p2tog; turn.

Row 22 Sl 1, k9, M1R, k1, sl marker, k15, sl marker, k1—28 sts (15 sts between markers form gusset). **Note** Final st from adjacent base triangle has not been worked.

Thumb

Place first st onto self-locking st marker; drop gusset marker. Place gusset sts onto larger dpns as follows: 3 sts on needle 1; 6 sts on needle 2; 6 sts on needle 3. Drop marker. Leave remaining sts on cable of circular needle to be worked later. Cast on 1 st onto needle 1—16 sts for thumb. Join and pm for beg of rnds. Work around in St st for 2¼"/5.5cm.

Dec rnd 1 *K1, k2tog; rep from * around to last st, end k1—11 sts.

Dec rnd 2 [K2tog] 5 times, k1—6 sts. Cut yarn leaving an 6"/15cm tail and thread through rem sts. Pull tog tightly and secure end. To finish diamond 1, slide rem sts from diamond 1 (resting on cable of circular needle) back onto needle, remove self-locking st marker from single st at base of thumb and place st with diamond 1 sts on circular needle. With WS facing, rejoin yarn, ssp, p10, p2tog—12 sts. Diamond 1 with thumb gusset is completed.

Diamond 2

Pull needle through diamond 1 sts so they are on cable and needle is free to work next diamond. With WS facing, pick up and p 12 sts along right edge of base triangle 2; turn.

*Row 1 (RS)** Sl 1, k11; turn.

Row 2 Sl 1, p10, p2tog (last st from diamond 2 and first st from base triangle 1); turn. Rep from * until all 12 sts from base triangle are worked, end with a WS row—12 sts.

Diamond 3

With WS facing, pick up and p 12 sts along left edge of diamond 1 (with thumb gusset); turn.

*Row 1 (RS)** Sl 1, k10, ssk (last st from diamond 3 and first st from diamond 2); turn.

Row 2 Sl 1, p11; turn. Rep from * until all 12 sts from diamond 2 are worked, end with a RS row—12 sts.

Diamond 4

Pull needle through so sts rest on cable and needle is free to work next diamond. With RS facing, pick up and k12 sts along left edge of diamond 2; turn. **Row 1 (WS)** Sl 1, p11; turn.

Row 2 Sl 1, k10, ssk; turn. Rep from * until all 12 sts from diamond 1 are worked, end with a RS row—12 sts.

Diamond 5

With RS facing, pick up and k 12 sts along right edge of diamond 3; turn. **Row 1 (WS)** Sl 1, p10, p2tog; turn.

Row 2 Sl 1, k11; turn. Rep from * until all 12 sts from diamond 4 are worked, end with a WS row—12 sts.

Diamond 6

Pull needle through so sts rest on cable and needle is free to work next diamond. With WS facing, pick up and p 12 sts along right edge of diamond 4; turn.

*Row 1 (RS)** Sl 1, k11; turn.

Row 2 Sl 1, p10, p2tog; turn. Rep from * until all 12 sts from diamond 3 are worked, end with a WS row—12 sts.

Diamond 7

With WS facing, pick up and p 12 sts along right edge of diamond 5; turn. **Row 1 (RS)** Sl 1, k10, ssk; turn.

Row 2 Sl 1, p11; turn. Rep from * until all 12 sts from diamond 6 are worked, end with a RS row—12 sts.

Diamond 8

Pull needle through so sts rest on cable and needle is free to work next diamond. With RS facing, pick up and k 12 sts along left edge of diamond 6; turn. **Row 1 (WS)** Sl 1, p11; turn.

Row 2 Sl 1, k10, ssk; turn. Rep from * until all 12 sts from diamond 5 are worked, end with a WS row—12 sts. Do not cut yarn.

Finishing

Turn mitten WS out, taking care not to drop any sts. Pull needle through so sts rest on cable and needle is free to work next sts. With WS of diamond 8 facing, pick up and p12 sts along right edge. With RS of diamonds 7 and 8 tog, use a larger dpn to work 3-needle bind-off. With WS of diamond 7 facing, pick up and p11 sts along edge—12 sts on needle. With RS tog, work 3-needle bind-off. Cut yarn and weave in ends. Turn RS out. ■

Cloche Hat

Cloche Hat

This charming cap is trimmed with a picot band that is picked up and knit, resulting in striking contrast of color.

Designed by Carol J. Sulcoski

Skill Level: ■■■□

Materials

- 2 1¾oz/50g skeins (each approx 110 yd/100m) of Noro *Kureyon* (wool) in #264 hot pink/lilac/brown/purple
- Contrasting worsted-weight yarn (waste yarn)
- Size 8 (5mm) circular needle, 16"/40cm long, OR SIZE TO OBTAIN GAUGE
- One set (5) size 8 (5mm) double-pointed needles (dpns)
- Size H/8 (5mm) crochet hook (for chain-st provisional cast-on)
- Stitch marker

Size
Instructions are written for one size.

Knitted Measurements
Head circumference 20¾"/53cm
Depth 7¾"/19.5cm

Gauge
16 sts and 24 rows to 4"/10cm over St st using size 8 (5mm) dpns.
TAKE TIME TO CHECK GAUGE.

Notes
1) Sides of hat are worked back and forth in a strip, then short edges are grafted together to form a tube.
2) Stitches are picked up around the top of the tube to form the crown, then around the bottom edge to form the brim.

Hat
Sides
With crochet hook and waste yarn, ch 20 for chain-st provisional cast-on. Cut yarn and draw end though lp on hook. Turn ch so bottom lps are at top and cut end is at left. With dpns, beg 2 lps from right end, pick up and k 1 st in each of next 15 lps —15 sts. Beg with a purl row, cont in St st working on 2 dpns until piece measures 21"/53.5cm from beg. Cut yarn leaving an 18"/45.5cm tail. With RS facing, release cut end from lp of waste yarn ch. Pulling out 1 ch at a time, place 15 live sts onto a 2nd dpn ready for a RS row. Graft sts tog using Kitchener st (see page 142).

Crown
With RS facing and circular needle, pick up and k 85 sts evenly spaced around one long edge of sides. Join and pm for beg of rnd. Cont in St st (knit every rnd) until piece measure 5½"/14cm from bottom edge of sides.

Crown Shaping

Change to dpns (dividing sts evenly between 4 needles) when there are too few sts on circular needle.

Dec rnd 1 K7, *SK2P, k14; rep from * around to last 10 sts, end SK2P, k7 —75 sts. Knit next rnd.

Dec rnd 2 K6, *SK2P, k12; rep from * around to last 9 sts, end SK2P, k6 —65 sts. Knit next rnd.

Dec rnd 3 K5, *SK2P, k10; rep from * around to last 8 sts, end SK2P, k5 —55 sts. Knit next rnd.

Dec rnd 4 K4, *SK2P, k8; rep from * around to last 7 sts, end SK2P, k4   45 sts. Knit next rnd.

Dec rnd 5 K3, *SK2P, k6; rep from * around to last 6 sts, end SK2P, k3 —35 sts. Knit next rnd.

Dec rnd 6 K2, *SK2P, k4; rep from * around to last 5 sts, end SK2P, k2 —25 sts. Knit next rnd.

Dec rnd 7 K1, *SK2P, k2; rep from * around to last 4 sts, end SK2P, k1   15 sts. Knit next rnd. Drop marker, place last st of last rnd on LH needle, pm for new beg of rnd.

Dec rnd 8 *SK2P, k1; rep from * around to last 3 sts, end SK2P —7 sts. Cut yarn leaving an 8"/20.5cm tail and thread through rem sts. Pull tog tightly and secure end.

Brim

With RS facing and circular needle, pick up and k 86 sts evenly spaced around opposite long edge of sides. Join and pm for beg of rnd.

Rnds 1 and 2 Purl.

Rnds 3–5 Knit.

Rnd (picot) 6 *K2tog, yo; rep from * around.

Rnds 7–10 Knit. Bind off all sts loosely knitwise. Cut yarn leaving a 30"76cm tail. Turn bottom edge of brim to WS along picot rnd and hem in place. ∎

Mitered Scarf

Mitered Scarf

Visually overlapping mitered squares and a ruffled edging create a festive wrap that will liven up any outfit.

Designed by Valentina Devine

Skill Level: ■■■□

Materials

■ 4 1¾oz/50g skeins (each approx 110 yd/100m) of Noro *Kureyon* (wool) in #226 red/teal/olive/magenta
■ One pair size 9 (5.5mm) needles OR SIZE TO OBTAIN GAUGE
■ Size H/8 (5mm) crochet hook

Size

Instructions are written for one size.

Knitted Measurements

Approx 7" x 37½"/18cm x 95cm (excluding ruffle)

Gauge

22 sts and 28 rows to 4"/10cm over garter st (knit every row) using size 9 (5.5mm) needles.
Each square measures 7" x 7½"/18cm x 19cm. TAKE TIME TO CHECK GAUGE.

Square A

Motif 1
Cast on 19 sts.
Row 1 (WS) K8, SK2P, k8—17 sts.
Row 2 and all RS rows to row 14 Knit.
Row 3 K7, SK2P, k7—15 sts.
Row 5 K6, SK2P, k6—13 sts.
Row 7 K5, SK2P, k5—11 sts.
Row 9 K4, SK2P, k4—9 sts.
Row 11 K3, SK2P, k3—7 sts.
Row 13 K2, SK2P, k2—5 sts.
Row 15 K1, SK2P, k1—3 sts.
Row 16 SK2P—1 st. *Do not cut yarn.* The st rem on needle counts as first st of motif 2.

Motif 2
With RS facing, pick up and 8 sts along side edge of motif 1 (9 sts on needle), then cast on 48 sts—57 sts.
Row 1 (WS) K8, SK2P, k16, SK2P, k16, SK2P, k8—51 sts.
Row 2 and all RS rows to row 16 Knit.
Row 3 K7, SK2P, k14, SK2P, k14, SK2P, k7—45 sts.
Row 5 K6, SK2P, k12, SK2P, k12, SK2P, k6—39 sts.
Row 7 K5, SK2P, k10, SK2P, k10, SK2P, k5—33 sts.
Row 9 K4, SK2P, k8, SK2P, k8, SK2P, k4—27 sts.
Row 11 K3, SK2P, k6, SK2P, k6, SK2P, k3—21 sts.
Row 13 K2, SK2P, k4, SK2P, k4, SK2P, k2—15 sts.
Row 15 K1, SK2P, k2, SK2P, k2, SK2P, k1—9 sts.
Row 17 [SK2P] 3 times—3 sts.
Row 18 SK2P—1 st. Cut yarn and fasten off last st.

Motif 3

Cast on 28 sts, then with RS facing, pick up and k 9 sts along top edge of motif 1, 10 sts along top inside edge of motif 2, then 10 sts along inside edge of motif 2—57 sts. Rep rows 1–18 of motif 2. Cut yarn and fasten off last st.

Motif 4

With RS facing, pick up and k 9 sts along inside edge of motif 3, 10 sts along top inside edge of motif 3, 10 sts along top edge of motif 2, then cast on 9 sts—38 sts.

Row 1 (WS) K8, SK2P, k16, SK2P, k8—34 sts.

Row 2 and all RS rows to row 16 Knit.

Row 3 K7, SK2P, k14, SK2P, k7—30 sts.

Row 5 K6, SK2P, k12, SK2P, k6—26 sts.

Row 7 K5, SK2P, k10, SK2P, k5—22 sts.

Row 9 K4, SK2P, k8, SK2P, k4—18 sts.

Row 11 K3, SK2P, k6, SK2P, k3—14 sts.

Row 13 K2, SK2P, k4, SK2P, k2—10 sts.

Row 15 K1, SK2P, k2, SK2P, k1—6 sts.

Row 17 [SK2P] twice—2 sts.

Row 18 K2tog—1 st. Cut yarn and fasten off last st.

Square B

Motif 1

Cast on 10 sts, then with RS facing, pick up and k 9 sts along top edge of motif 3 of square A—19 sts. Rep rows 1–16 of motif 1 of square A. *Do not cut yarn.* The st rem on needle counts as first st of motif 2.

Motif 2

With RS facing, pick up and k 8 sts along side edge of motif 1 (9 sts on needle), then pick up and k 20 sts along top edge of motif 4 of square A, then cast on 28 sts—57 sts. Rep rows 1–18 of motif 2 of square A.

Motifs 3 and 4

Work same as for square A.

Square C

Cast on 10 sts, then with RS facing, pick up and k 9 sts along top edge of motif 3 of square B—19 sts. Rep rows 1–16 of motif 1 of square A. *Do not cut yarn.* The st rem on needle counts as first st of motif 2.

Motif 2

With RS facing, pick up and k 8 sts along side edge of motif 1 (9 sts on needle), then pick up and k 20 sts along top edge of motif 4 of square B, then cast on 28 sts—57 sts. Rep rows 1–18 of motif 2 of square A.

Motifs 3 and 4

Work same as for square A.

Square D

Cast on 10 sts, then with RS facing, pick up and k 9 sts along top edge of motif 3 of square C—19 sts. Rep rows 1–16 of motif 1 of square A. *Do not cut yarn.* The st rem on needle counts as first st of motif 2.

Motif 2

With RS facing, pick up and k 8 sts along side edge of motif 1 (9 sts on needle), then pick up and k 20 sts along top edge of motif 4 of square C, then cast on 28 sts—57 sts. Rep rows 1–18 of motif 2 of square A.

Motifs 3 and 4

Work same as for square A.

Square E

Cast on 10 sts, then with RS facing, pick up and k 9 sts along top edge of motif 3 of square D—19 sts. Rep rows 1–16 of motif 1 of square A. *Do not cut yarn.* The st rem on needle counts as first st of motif 2.

Motif 2

With RS facing, pick up and k 8 sts along side edge of motif 1 (9 sts on needle), then pick up and k 20 sts along top edge of motif 4 of square D, then cast on 28 sts—57 sts. Rep rows 1–18 of motif 2 of square A.

Motifs 3 and 4

Work same as for square A.

Finishing

Block piece lightly to measurements.

Ruffle

With RS facing and crochet hook, join yarn with a sl st in top LH corner of scarf.

Rnd 1 (RS) Ch 1, making sure that work lies flat, sc evenly around entire outer edge, working 2 sc in each corner, join rnd with a sl st in first sc. Turn.

Row 1 (WS) Ch 4, work 2 tr in each sc along first short edge, next long edge, then 2nd short edge to next corner. Turn.

Row 2 Ch 4, tr in each tr to end. Fasten off. ∎

(Diagram on page 139)

Tea Cozy

Tea Cozy

Warm up your tabletop with the vibrant autumn colors of this cheery cozy.

Designed by Linda Medina

Skill Level: ■■■□

Materials
- 2 1¾oz/50g skeins (each approx 110 yd/100m) of Noro *Kureyon* (wool) in #95 lime/hot pink/orange
- Contrasting worsted-weight yarn (waste yarn)
- Matching sport-weight yarn (for sewing)
- One pair size 7 (4.5mm) needles OR SIZE TO OBTAIN GAUGE
- Spare size 7 (4.5mm) needle
- Size 6 (4mm) circular needle, 16"/40cm long
- Two size 6 (4mm) double-pointed needles (dpns) for I-cords
- Size H/8 (5mm) crochet hook (for chain-st provisional cast-on)
- Stitch marker

Size
Sized to fit a 6-cup teapot.

Knitted Measurements
Circumference approx 16"/40.5cm (unstretched)
Height approx 10"/25.5cm (excluding fringe)

Gauge
22 sts and 22 rnds to 4"/10cm over pat st using size 7 (4.5mm) needles (unstretched). TAKE TIME TO CHECK GAUGE.

Note
I-cord fringe at top and ribbing at bottom edges are worked after body is completed.

Stitch Glossary
yb Yarn over needle from *front to back*.
yf Yarn over needle from *back to front*.

Pattern Stitch
(over a multiple of 5 sts plus 2)
Row 1 (RS) P2, *yb, k2tog tbl, k1, p2; rep from * to end.
Row 2 K2, *yf, k2tog tbl, p1, k2; rep from * to end.
Rep rows 1 and 2 for pat st.

Tea Cozy Body
Section I
With crochet hook and waste yarn, ch 52 for chain-st provisional cast-on. Cut yarn and draw end though lp on hook. Turn ch so bottom lps are at top and cut end is at left. With straight needles, beg 2 lps from right end, pick up and k 1 st in each of next 47 lps—47 sts. Rep rows 1 and 2 of pat st 8 times (16 rows). Cut yarn. Leave sts on spare needle.

Section II
Work same as section I; do not cut yarn.

Joining Sections
Row 17 (RS) Section II: Work row 1 of pat st to last 2 sts, p2tog; section I: P2tog, work row 1 of pat st to end—92 sts.
Row 18 Rep row 2.

Rows 19–24 Rep rows 1 and 2 three times.

Row 25 (RS) P2tog, *yb, k2tog tbl, k1, p2; rep from * to last 2 sts, p2tog—90 sts. Mark last row for handle opening.

Row 26 K1, *yf, k2tog tbl, p1, k2; rep from * across, ending last rep k1.

Row 27 P1, *yb, k2tog tbl, k1, p2; rep from * across, ending last rep k1.

Rows 28–57 Rep rows 26 and 27 fifteen times, then row 26 once. Change to circular needle.

Row 59 (RS) Purl. Leave sts on needle.

I-Cord Fringe

With WS facing, place first 3 sts on circular needle onto a dpn. Work in I-cord as foll: ***Next row (RS)** With 2nd dpn, k3, do not turn. Slide sts back to beg of needle to work next row from RS; rep from * for 3 ½"/9cm. **Next row** K2tog, k1, pass 2nd st over first st— 1 st. Cut yarn leaving a 6"/15cm end. Fasten off last st. Weave in end. *Place next 3 sts on dpn. Join yarn. Work I-cord same as first fringe. * Rep from * to * 28 times more (30 fringes).

Finishing

Using matching sport-weight yarn, sew side seam to marker for top of handle opening, or adjust seam length to fit your teapot. On WS, tack tog bottom edges of spout opening and handle opening.

Ribbing

With RS facing and working one section at a time, release cut end from lp of waste yarn ch. Pulling out 1 ch at a time, place 94 live sts onto circular needle ready for a RS rnd. Join yarn and pm for beg of rnds. **Next (dec) rnd** Knit, dec 6 sts evenly spaced—88 sts. Cont in k2, p2 rib for 6 rnds. Bind off in rib.

I-Cord Tie

With dpns, cast on 3 sts leaving a 6"/15cm tail. Work in I-cord same as fringe for 28"/71cm. Next row K2tog, k1, pass 2nd st over first st— 1 st. Cut yarn leaving a 6"/15cm end. Fasten off last st; weave in end. Weave in tail at opposite end. Place tea cozy on work surface, so spout opening is at left and handle opening is at right. Measure 2"/5cm down from top edge, then measure and mark for center. Beg and ending approx ¾"/2cm from each side of center mark, weave tie through pat st eyelets 2"/5cm below top edge. Knot each end of tie and each I cord fringe. Pull tie to gather in top edge, then tie in a bow. ∎

Curving Wrap

Curving Wrap

This unusual scarf curves gently, creating a snuggly cover-up to hug you close on the coldest of winter days.

Designed by Kathy Merrick

Skill Level: ■■■□

Materials

- 3 3½oz/100g hanks (each approx 131 yd/120m) of Noro *Iro* (wool/silk) in #99 orange/pink/brown/green
- One pair size 10 (6mm) needles OR SIZE TO OBTAIN GAUGE

Size

Instructions are written for one size.

Knitted Measurements

Approx 8½" (at widest point) x 83"/21.5cm x 210.5cm

Gauge

13 sts and 20 rows to 4"/10cm over St st (k on RS, p on WS) using size 10 (6mm) needles. TAKE TIME TO CHECK GAUGE.

Note

Shaping is done with short rows, *without* wraps.

Scarf

Cast on 24 sts. Work in garter st (knit every row) for 4 rows.

Section I
Rows 1 and 3 (RS) K23; turn.
Rows 2 and 4 P19, k4; turn.
Rows 5 and 7 K22; turn.
Rows 6 and 8 P18, k4; turn.
Rows 9 and 11 K21; turn.
Rows 10 and 12 P17, k4; turn.
Rows 13 and 15 K20; turn.
Rows 14 and 16 P16, k4; turn.
Rows 17 and 19 K19; turn.
Rows 18 and 20 P15, k4; turn.
Rows 21 and 23 K18; turn.
Rows 22 and 24 P14, k4; turn.
Rows 25 and 27 K17; turn.
Rows 26 and 28 P13, k4; turn.

Rows 29 and 31 K16; turn.
Rows 30 and 32 P12, k4; turn.
Rows 33 and 35 K15; turn.
Rows 34 and 36 P11, k4; turn.
Rows 37 and 39 K14; turn.
Rows 38 and 40 P10, k4; turn.
Rows 41 and 43 K13; turn.
Rows 42 and 44 P9, k4; turn.
Rows 45 and 47 K12; turn.
Rows 46 and 48 P8, k4; turn.
Rows 49 and 51 K11; turn.
Rows 50 and 52 P7, k4; turn.
Rows 53 and 55 K10; turn.
Rows 54 and 56 P6, k4; turn.
Rows 57 and 59 K9; turn.
Rows 58 and 60 P5, k4; turn.
Rows 61 and 63 K8; turn.
Rows 62 and 64 P4, k4; turn.
Rows 65 and 67 K7; turn.
Rows 66 and 68 P3, k4; turn.
Rows 69 and 71 K6; turn.
Rows 70 and 72 P2, k4; turn.
Rows 73 and 75 K5; turn.
Rows 74 and 76 P1, k4; turn.
Rows 77 and 78 K4; turn.
Row 79 (RS) K24 sts on LH needle; turn.

Section II
Rows 1 and 3 (WS) K4, p19; turn.
Rows 2 and 4 K23; turn.
Rows 5 and 7 K4, p18; turn.
Rows 6 and 8 K22; turn.
Rows 9 and 11 K4, p17; turn.
Rows 10 and 12 K21; turn.
Rows 13 and 15 K4, p16; turn.
Rows 14 and 16 K20; turn.
Rows 17 and 19 K4, p15; turn.

Rows 18 and 20 K19; turn.

Rows 21 and 23 K4, p14; turn.

Rows 22 and 24 K18; turn.

Rows 25 and 27 K4, p13; turn.

Rows 26 and 28 K17; turn.

Rows 29 and 31 K4, p12; turn.

Rows 30 and 32 K16; turn.

Rows 33 and 35 K4, p11; turn.

Rows 34 and 36 K15; turn.

Rows 37 and 39 K4, p10; turn.

Rows 38 and 40 K14; turn.

Rows 41 and 43 K4, p9; turn.

Rows 42 and 44 K13; turn.

Rows 45 and 47 K4, p8; turn.

Rows 46 and 48 K12; turn.

Rows 49 and 51 K4, p7; turn.

Rows 50 and 52 K11; turn.

Rows 53 and 55 K4, p6; turn.

Rows 54 and 56 K10; turn.

Rows 57 and 59 K4, p5; turn.

Rows 58 and 60 K9; turn.

Rows 61 and 63 K4, p4; turn.

Rows 62 and 64 K8; turn.

Rows 65 and 67 K4, p3; turn.

Rows 66 and 68 K7; turn.

Rows 69 and 71 K4, p2; turn.

Rows 70 and 72 K6; turn.

Rows 73 and 75 K4, p1; turn.

Rows 74 and 76 K5; turn.

Rows 77 and 78 K4; turn.

Row 79 (WS) K4, then p 20 sts on LH needle; turn. Rep sections I and II four times more. Work in garter st for 4 rows. Bind off knitwise.

Finishing

Block lightly to measurements. ∎

Leg Warmers

Leg Warmers

Channel your inner ballerina when you wear these lacy leg warmers knit in shades of pale blue, brown and green.

Designed by Judy Sumner

Skill Level: ■■■□

Materials

- 1 3½oz/100g skein (approx 328 yd/300m) of Noro *Silk Garden Sock Yarn* (lamb's wool/silk/nylon/kid mohair) in #268 green/aqua/brown
- One set (5) size 4 (3.5mm) double-pointed needles (dpns) OR SIZE TO OBTAIN GAUGE
- Stitch markers

Size

Instructions are written for one size.

Knitted Measurements

Circumference (around ankle) approx 8"/20.5cm
Circumference (around calf) approx 10½"/26.5cm
Length approx 17"/43cm

Gauge

24 sts and 30 rnds to 4"/10cm over chart pat using size 4 (3.5mm) dpns.
TAKE TIME TO CHECK GAUGE.

Note

To work in the rnd, always read chart from right to left.

Stitch Glossary

kf&b Inc 1 by knitting into the front and back of the next st.

Leg Warmer (make 2)

Cast on 48 sts. Divide sts over 4 needles. Join and pm taking care not to twist sts on needles. Work in k2, p2 rib for 1"/2.5cm.

Beg Chart Pat

Rnd 1 Work 12-st rep 4 times. Cont to foll chart in this way to rnd 16, then rep rnds 1–16 once more, then rnds 1–7 once.

Leg Shaping

Rnd (inc) 8 With beg of rnd marker on RH needle, M1, pm, knit to end of rnd—49 sts. Keeping 1 st between markers in St st, cont to foll chart rnds 9–15.

Rnd (inc) 16 With beg of rnd marker on RH needle, kf&b, sl marker, knit to end of rnd—50 sts. Keeping 2 sts between markers in St st, cont to foll chart rnds 1–7.

Rnd (inc) 8 With beg of rnd marker on RH needle, [kf&b] twice, sl marker, knit to end of rnd—52 sts. Keeping 4 sts between markers in St st, cont to foll chart rnds 9–15.

Rnd (inc) 16 With beg of rnd marker on RH needle, k1, [kf&b]

twice, k1, sl marker, knit to end of rnd—54 sts. Keeping 6 sts between markers in St st, cont to foll chart rnds 1–7.

Rnd (inc) 8 With beg of rnd marker on RH needle, k2, [kf&b] twice, k2, sl marker, knit to end of rnd—56 sts. Keeping 8 sts between markers in St st, cont to foll chart rnds 9–15.

Rnd (inc) 16 With beg of rnd marker on RH needle, k3, [kf&b] twice, k3, sl marker, knit to end of rnd—58 sts. Keeping 10 sts between markers in St st, cont to foll chart rnds 1–7.

Rnd (inc) 8 With beg of rnd marker on RH needle, k4, [kf&b] twice, k4, sl marker, knit to end of rnd—60 sts. Keeping 12 sts between markers in St st, cont to foll chart rnds 9–15.

Rnd (inc) 16 With beg of rnd marker on RH needle, k5, [kf&b] twice, k5, sl marker, knit to end of rnd—62 sts. Keeping 14 sts between markers in St st, cont to foll chart rnds 1–7.

Rnd (inc) 8 With beg of rnd marker on RH needle, k6, [kf&b] twice, k6, sl marker, knit to end of rnd—64 sts. Keeping 16 sts between markers in St st, cont to foll chart rnds 9–16. Work in k2, p2 rib for 1½"/4cm. Bind off loosely in rib.

Finishing

Block pieces lightly to measurements. ■

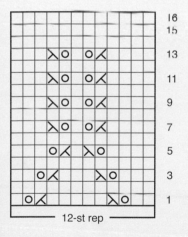

12-st rep

Stitch Key

☐   Knit

◎   Yarn over

☒   K2tog

☒   Ssk

Diamond-Motif Shawl

Diamond-Motif Shawl

The soft colors of peat moss and heather and a touch of sky blue bring the feeling of the Highlands to this lovely little wrap.

Designed by Valentina Devine

Skill Level: ■■■□

Materials

- 3 1¾oz/50g skeins (each approx 110 yd/100m) of Noro *Silk Garden* (silk/kid mohair/lamb's wool) in #272 grey/lime/brown/purple
- One pair size 7 (4.5mm) needles, OR SIZE TO OBTAIN GAUGE
- Size E/4 (3.5mm) crochet hook
- Stitch markers

Size

Instructions are written for one size.

Knitted Measurements

Width approx 39"/99cm (excluding fringe)
Length approx 17"/43cm (excluding fringe)

Gauge

18 sts and 24 rows to 4"/10cm over rib pat using size 7 (4.5mm) needles. TAKE TIME TO CHECK GAUGE.
Each full motif measures approx 4½"/11.5cm wide and 4"/10cm long.

Shawl

Refer to diagram for placement of motifs and where to cast on and pick up sts.

Motif 1
Cast on 26 sts.
Row 1 (WS) Sl 1 purlwise, k2, [p2, k2] twice, k2tog, place marker, p1, k1, [p2, k2] twice, p2, k1 tbl—25 sts.
Row 2 (RS) Sl 1 purlwise, k2, [p2, k2] twice, k2tog, slip marker, (sm), p1, [p2, k2] twice, p2, k1 tbl—24 sts. Place marker on this row to indicate RS.
Row 3 Sl 1 purlwise, work in k2, p2 rib as established (k the knit sts and p the purl sts) to 2 sts before marker, k2tog, sm, p1, work in rib as established to last st, k1 tbl—23 sts.
Rows 4–19 Rep row 3 sixteen times—7 sts.
Row 20 (RS) Sl 1 purlwise, k1, k2tog, sm, p2, k1 tbl—6 sts.
Row 21 Sl 1 purlwise, k2tog, sm, p2, k1 tbl—5 sts.
Row 22 Sl 1 purlwise, k2tog, sm, p1, k1 tbl—4 sts.
Row 24 K2tog, sm, p1, k1 tbl—3 sts.
Row 25 K2tog, sm, k1 tbl—2 sts.
Row 24 K2tog—1 st. Fasten off.
Note When picking up sts along RH edge of motifs, work into the first st of row; when picking up sts along LH edge of motifs, work into the last st of row.
Motif 2
Cast on 13 sts, then with RS facing, pick up and k 13 sts evenly spaced along top RH edge of motif 1—26 sts. Rep rows 1–25 of motif 1.
Motif 3
With RS facing, pick up and k 13 sts evenly spaced along top LH edge of motif 1, then turn to WS and cast 13 sts onto same needle; do not turn—26 sts. Rep rows 1–25 of motif 1.
Motif 4
Cast on 13 sts, then with RS facing, pick up and k 13 sts evenly spaced along top RH edge of motif 2—26 sts. Rep rows 1–25 of motif 1.
Motif 5
With RS facing, pick up and k 13 sts evenly spaced along top LH

edge of motif 2, then 13 sts along top RH edge of motif 3—26 sts. Rep rows 1–25 of motif 1.

Motif 6
With RS facing, pick up and k 13 sts evenly spaced along top LH edge of motif 3, then turn to WS and cast 13 sts onto same needle; do not turn—26 sts. Rep rows 1–25 of motif 1.

Motifs 7–28
Referring to diagram for placement of motifs, work motifs 7, 11, 16, 22 same as motif 4; work motifs 10, 15, 21, 28 same as motif 6; work rem center motifs same as motif 5.

Triangles
The LH edge of triangles 1–7 are picked up along the top RH edge of motifs 22–28. This is done by picking up 1 st in RH edge every RS row, then this extra st is dec on the foll WS row. Take care to pick up sts evenly.

Triangle 1
Cast on 13 sts, then with RS facing, pick up and k 1 st in first row of RH edge of motif 22—14 sts.

Row 1 (WS) K2tog, [k2, p2] 3 times—13 sts.

Row (dec) 2 (RS) K2tog, work in k2, p2 rib to end, then pick up and k 1 st in next row of RH edge of motif 22—13 sts.

Row 3 K2tog, work in rib to end—12 sts. Rep rows 2 and 3 until 1 st rem. Fasten off last st.

Triangle 2
With RS facing, pick up and k 13 sts along top LH edge of motif 22,

then pick up and k 1 st in first row of RH edge of motif 23—14 sts. Beg with row 1, cont to work same as triangle 1.

Triangles 3–7
Referring to diagram, work same as triangle 2.

Triangle 8
With RS facing, pick up and k 13 sts evenly spaced along top LH edge of motif 28.

Row 1 (WS) K3, [p2, k2] twice, p2.

Row (dec) 2 (RS) K2tog, work in rib to end—12 sts.

Row 3 Work in rib to end. Rep rows 2 and 3 until 1 st rem. Fasten off.

Finishing
Block piece lightly to measurements.

Edging and Fringe
With RS facing and crochet hook, join yarn with a sl st in LH corner of triangle 8.

Rnd 1 (RS) Ch 1, making sure that work lies flat, sc evenly around entire outer edge, working 3 sc in each corner, join rnd with a sl st in first sc. *Do not turn; do not fasten off.* Work fringe as foll:

Next row (RS) Ch 15, sl st in next sc, *ch 1, sl st in next sc, ch 15, sl st in same sc; rep from * along both angled edges of shawl. Fasten off. Work reverse sc across top edge as foll: With RS facing, join yarn with a sl st in first sc at top LH corner of triangle 1.

Next row (RS) Ch 1, working from left to right, sc in each sc to end. Fasten off. ■

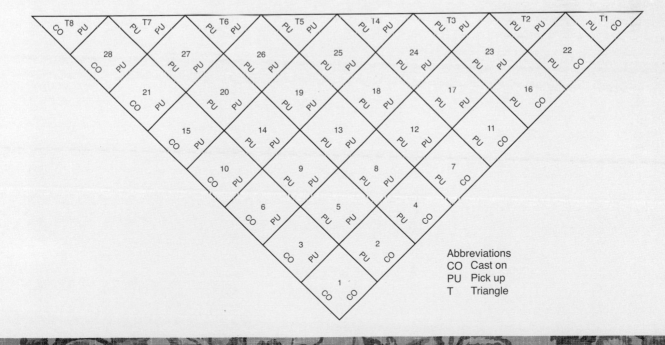

Abbreviations
CO Cast on
PU Pick up
T   Triangle

Dog Sweater

Dog Sweater

This sporty number will give your best pal added warmth on winter walks. The neck adjusts with a drawstring for an easy fit.

Designed by Astor Tsang

Skill Level: ■■■□

Materials

- 3 3½oz/100g hanks (each approx 165 yd/151m) of Noro *Kogarashi* (silk/wool) each in #10 purple/turquoise/hot pink
- Size 10 (6mm) circular needles, 16"/41cm and 24"/61cm long, OR SIZE TO OBTAIN GAUGE
- One set (4) size 8 (5mm) double-pointed needles (dpns)
- Stitch markers
- One 48"/114cm long black shoe lace

Sizes

Instructions are written for a 40- to 60-pound Medium-size dog.

Knitted Measurements

Neck circumference approx 18"/45.5cm (unstretched)
Chest circumference approx 24"/61cm (unstretched)
Length approx 20"/51cm (excluding turtleneck)

Gauge

14 sts and 20 rnds to 4"/10cm over St st (knit every rnd) using size 10 (6mm) circular needle. TAKE TIME TO CHECK GAUGE.

Note

Sweater is made in one piece from the neck down.

Stitch Glossary

kf&b Inc 1 by knitting into the front and back of the next st.

Body

Turtleneck

With shorter circular needle, cast on 72 sts. Join taking care not to twist sts on needle, pm for beg of rnds. Work around in k2, p2 rib for 7½"/19cm.

Next (leash opening) rnd Work in k2, p2 rib for 46 sts, bind off next 4 sts, work in rib to end.

Next rnd Work in k2, p2 rib for 46 sts, cast on 4 sts, work in k2, p2 rib to end. Cont to work even until piece measures 9½"/24cm from beg.

Chest

Rnd 1 K22, pm (2nd marker), beg with k2, work k2, p2 rib to end of rnd. **Note** Rib pat has now been reversed.

Rnd (inc) 2 K1, kf&b, knit to 2 sts before marker, M1, k2, sl marker, work in rib to end—74 sts. Change to longer circular needle.

Rnd 3 Knit to marker, sl marker, work in rib to end. Rep rnds 2 and 3 twelve times more—98 sts.

Leg openings

Next row (RS) K13, join a 2nd ball of yarn and with shorter circular needle, k22 for center panel; turn. Leave rem 76 sts on longer circular needle for back. Beg with a purl row, work back and forth in St st on center 22 sts for 15 rows more, end with a WS row. Cut yarn. Leave 22 sts on shorter circular needle. Return to longer circular needle. Beg with a WS row, work back and forth in pat sts as established for 14 rows, end with a RS row.

Next (joining) rnd (RS) With longer circular needle, k22 from center panel needle, work to end of rnd. Work even in established pat sts for 1"/2.5cm.

Underbelly

Next rnd K2, *p1, k1; rep from * to 2 sts before marker, k2, sl marker, work in k2, p2 rib, end k2.

Next (dec) rnd K1, SKP, work in k1, p1 rib to 3 sts before marker, k2tog, k1, sl marker, work in k2, p2 rib, end k2. Rep last rnd 4 times more—88 sts. Work even in pat sts as established until underbelly measures approx 7½"/18.5cm from beg of leg openings.

Next rnd Bind off loosely in pat sts to marker, drop marker, work in k2, p2 rib, end k2—50 sts. Turn. Work back and forth in k2, p2 rib until piece measures approx 20"/51cm from last rnd of turtleneck. Bind off in rib.

Finishing

Do not block.

Leg opening trim

With RS facing and first dpn, beg along the top of the leg opening, pick up and k 15 sts along one side, then with a 2nd dpn, pick up and k 15 sts along opposite side—30 sts. Divide sts evenly between 3 needles. Join and pm for beg of rnds. Knit next 5 rnds. Bind off loosely knitwise. Rep for 2nd leg opening. Beg and ending on side opposite leash opening, thread shoelace under and over rib sts around neck, just below leash opening. ■

Long Lace Scarf

Long Lace Scarf

This generously sized muffler knit in earth tones exudes warmth, while the subtle lace pattern keeps it from being too heavy.

Designed by Tanis Gray

Skill Level: ■■□□

Materials

- 3 3½oz/100g hanks (each approx 131 yd/120m) of Noro *Iro* (wool/silk) in #57 brown/green/purple/cherry/pink
- One pair size 10 (6mm) needles OR SIZE TO OBTAIN GAUGE

Size

Instructions are written for one size

Knitted Measurements

Approx 8½" x 110"/21.5cm x 279.5cm

Gauge

16 sts and 19 rows to 5"/12.5cm over chart pat using size 10 (6mm) needles. TAKE TIME TO CHECK GAUGE.

Scarf

Cast on 27 sts.

Beg Chart Pat

Row 1 (RS) Work first st, work 6-st rep 4 times, work last 2 sts. Cont to foll chart in this way to row 12, then rep rows 1–12 thirty-four times more, or until there are 3 yd/2.75m of yarn rem, end with a WS row. Bind off knitwise.

Finishing

Block piece lightly to measurements. ∎

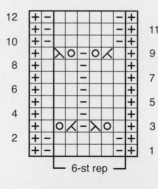

Stitch Key

☐	Knit on RS, purl on WS
−	Purl on RS, knit on WS
+	Knit on RS, knit on WS
O	Yarn over
⧄	K2tog
⧅	Ssk

6-st rep

Cabled Mittens

Cabled Mittens

Classically stylish and rich with texture, these handsome handwarmers will be your constant cold-weather companions.

Designed by Debbie O'Neill

Skill Level: ■■■□

Materials
- 2 1¾oz/50g skeins (each approx 110 yd/100m) of Noro *Silk Garden* (silk/kid mohair/lamb's wool) in #211 turquoise/fuchsia
- One set (5) size 4 (3.5mm) double-pointed needles (dpns) OR SIZE TO OBTAIN GAUGE
- Cable needle (cn)
- Stitch markers
- Scrap yarn

Size
Instructions are written for one size.

Knitted Measurements
Hand circumference 7 ½"/19cm
Length of cuff approx 3"/7.5cm

Gauge
21 sts and 28 rnds to 4"/10cm over St st using size 4 (3.5mm) dpns.
TAKE TIME TO CHECK GAUGE.

Note
To work in the rnd, always read chart from right to left.

Stitch Glossary
2-st RT K2tog leaving sts on LH needle, k first st again, sl both sts from needle.
2-st LT With RH needle behind LH needle, skip the first st and k 2nd st tbl, insert RH needle into backs of both sts, k2tog tbl.
6-st RC Sl 3 sts to cn and hold to *back*, k3, k3 from cn.
6-st LC Sl 3 sts to cn and hold to *front*, k3, k3 from cn.

Baby Cable Rib
(over a multiple of 4 sts)
Rnds 1 and 2 *K2, p2; rep from * around.
Rnd 3 *2-st RT, p2; rep from * around.
Rnd 4 Rep rnd 1.
Rep rnds 1–4 for baby cable rib.

Right Mitten
Cuff
Cast on 48 sts. Divide sts over 4 needles. Join taking care not to twist sts on needles, pm for beg of rnds. Work in baby cable rib for 3"/7.5cm.
Next (inc) rnd K11, p1, k4, p1, k1, p1, k4, M1, k4, p1, k1, p1, k4, p1, k13—49 sts.
Beg chart pat
Rnd 1 K11, work chart over next 25 sts, k13. Keeping sts each side of chart in St st (k every rnd), cont to foll chart in this way through rnd 4.
Thumb gusset
Rnd (inc) 5 K11, work chart over next 25 sts, k1, pm, M1, k1, M1, pm, knit to end of rnd—51 sts (3 sts between gusset markers).
Rnd 6 Work around in established pats.
Rnd (inc) 7 K11, work chart over next 25 sts, k1, sl marker, M1, knit to marker, M1, sl marker, knit to end of rnd—53 sts (5 sts between gusset markers).

Rnd 8 Work around in established pats. Beg chart on rnd 1 again, cont to inc 2 sts between gusset markers on next rnd, then every other rnd 5 times more, end with rnd 4—65 sts (17 sts between gusset markers).

Next rnd K11, work chart rnd 5 over next 25 sts, k1, place next 17 sts on scrap yarn for thumb (dropping markers), cast on 3 sts, knit to end of rnd—51 sts.

Hand

Rnd 6 K11, work chart over next 25 sts, k15. Keeping sts each side of chart pat in St st, cont to work even through rnd 8, then rep rnds 1–8 until piece measures 8"/20.5cm from beg.

Top shaping

Next (set-up) rnd K9, pm, k2, pm, work 25 sts in chart pat as established, pm, k2, pm, knit to end. **Note** There will be 3 more sts on the back of the hand than there are on the palm.

Next (dec) rnd Knit to 2 sts before marker, ssk, sl marker, k2, sl marker, k2tog, work in chart pat as established to 2 sts before next marker, ssk, sl marker, k2, sl marker, k2tog, knit to end. Work next rnd even. Rep last 2 rnds 6 times more, then dec rnd only once—19 sts (8 sts on palm and 11 sts back of the hand).

Next (dec) rnd Knit to 2nd marker, dec 3 sts evenly spaced to 3rd marker, knit to end of rnd—16 sts (8 sts on palm and 8 sts on back of hand).

Next row K to one st after first marker, then place 8 sts of back of hand on one needle and 8 sts of palm on 2nd needle. Cut yarn leaving a long tail for sewing. Graft top sts closed using Kitchener stitch (page 142).

Thumb

Place 17 thumb gusset sts over 2 needles.

Next rnd Join yarn and knit across sts, then pick up and k 3 st over cast-on of thumb opening—20 sts. Divide sts evenly over 3 needles. Join and pm for beg of rnds. Cont in St st for 1¼"/3cm.

Top shaping

Next (dec) rnd *K2tog, k1; rep from * around to last 2 sts, end k2tog—13 sts. Work next rnd even.

Next (dec) rnd [K2tog] 6 times, k1—7 sts. Cut yarn leaving a 6"/15cm tail and thread through rem sts. Pull tog tightly and secure end.

Left Mitten

Cuff

Work same as right mitten—49 sts.

Beg chart pat

Rnd 1 K11, work chart over next 25 sts, k13. Keeping sts each side of chart in St st, cont to foll chart in this way through rnd 4.

Thumb gusset

Rnd (inc) 5 K9, pm, M1, k1, M1, pm, k1, work chart over next 25 sts, knit to end of rnd—51 sts (3 sts between gusset markers).

Rnd 6 Work around in established pats. **Rnd (inc) 7** K9, sl marker, M1, knit to marker, M1, sl marker, work chart over next 25 sts, knit to end of rnd—53 sts (5 sts between gusset markers).

Rnd 8 Work around in established pats. Beg chart on rnd 1 again, cont to inc 2 sts between gusset markers on next rnd, then every other rnd 5 times more, end with rnd 4—65 sts (17 sts between gusset markers).

Next rnd K9, place next 17 sts on scrap yarn for thumb (dropping markers), cast on 3 sts, work to end of rnd—51 sts.

Hand

Rnd 6 K13, work chart over next 25 sts, k13. Keeping sts each side of chart pat in St st, cont to work even through rnd 8, then rep rnds 1–8 until piece measures 8"/20.5cm from beg.

Top shaping

Next (set-up) rnd K11, pm, k2, pm, work 25 sts in chart pat as established, pm, k2, pm, knit to end. **Note** There will be 3 more sts on the back of the hand than there are on the palm.

Next (dec) rnd Knit to 2 sts before marker, ssk, sl marker, k2, sl marker, k2tog, work in chart pat as established to 2 sts before next marker, ssk, sl marker, k2, sl marker, k2tog, knit to end. Work next rnd even. Rep last 2 rnds 6 times more, then dec rnd only once—19 sts (8 sts on palm and 11 sts back of the hand).

Next (dec) rnd Knit to 2nd marker, dec 3 sts evenly spaced to 3rd marker, knit to end of rnd—16 sts (8 sts on palm and 8 sts on back of hand).

Next row Knit to one st after first marker, then place k8 sts of back of hand on one needle and 8 sts of palm on a 2nd needle. Cut yarn leaving a long tail for sewing. Graft top sts closed using Kitchener stitch.

Thumb

Work same as right mitten. ∎

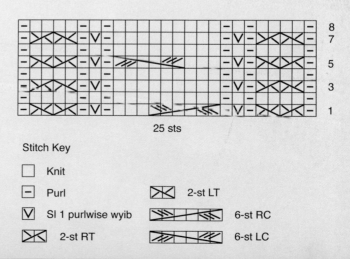

25 sts

Stitch Key

☐ Knit

⊟ Purl

Ⅴ Sl 1 purlwise wyib

⬅ 2-st RT

⬅ 2-st LT

6-st RC

6-st LC

Felted Entrelac Bag

Felted Entrelac Bag

This little pouch is the perfect size to hold your keys, cards and other necessities for a day of shopping or a night out on the town.

Designed by Erica Schlueter

Skill Level: ■■■■

Materials

■ 2 1¾oz/50g skeins (each approx 110 yd/100m)of Noro *Kureyon* (wool) in #262 grey/black/brown/rust
■ One pair size 8 (5mm) needles OR SIZE TO OBTAIN GAUGE
■ Two size 8 (5mm) double-pointed needles (dpns) for I-cord strap
■ Size I/9 (5.5mm) crochet hook

Size
Instructions are written for one size.

Knitted Measurements
Approx 5¼"/13.5cm wide x 7¼"/18.5cm high (after felting; excluding 60"/152.5cm long strap)

Gauge
14 sts and 19 rows to 4"/10cm over St st (k on RS, p on WS) using size 8 (5mm) needles (before felting). TAKE TIME TO CHECK GAUGE.

Note
Front, back and flap are made in one piece.

Stitch Glossary
kf&b Inc 1 by knitting into the front and back of the next st.

Bag
Beg at top edge of front (and ending at bottom edge of flap), with straight needles, cast on 18 sts.
Base triangles
*Row 1 (RS) K1; turn.
Row 2 and all WS rows Purl the same number of sts worked in the previous row; turn.
Row 3 Sl 1, k1; turn.
Row 5 Sl 1, k2; turn.
Row 7 Sl 1, k3; turn.
Row 9 Sl 1, k4; turn.
Row 11 Sl 1, k5. *Do not turn.* Rep from * twice more—3 base triangles completed. **Note** Make sure when starting next triangle not to work across sts of previous triangle.
Left-edge triangle (when RS is facing)
Row 1 (WS) P1; turn.
Row 2 Kf&b; turn.
Row 3 P1, p2tog; turn.
Row 4 K1, M1, k1; turn.
Row 5 P2, p2tog; turn.
Row 6 and all RS rows Knit to last st, M1, k1; turn.

Row 7 P3, p2tog; turn.

Row 9 P4, p2tog; turn.

Row 11 P5, p2tog (you should have 6 worked sts on RH needle). *Do not turn.*

Right-slanting rectangles (when RS is facing)

Row 1 (WS) With WS facing, pick up and purl 6 sts along slip st edge of foundation triangle (for later rectangles it will be from left-slanting rectangle row). Be sure to pick up both parts of slipped st, it will look like 2 sts on the needle. Sl last picked up st back on LH needle and p2tog. Turn.

Row 2 K6; turn.

Row 3 Sl 1, p4, p2tog; turn.

Rows 4–11 Rep rows 2 and 3 four times more; after row 11 *do not turn.* Work one more rectangle, then work right edge triangle as foll:

Right-edge triangle (when RS is facing)

Row 1 (WS) With WS facing, pick up and purl 6 sts along slip st edge of foundation triangle, (for later triangles it will be from left-slanting rectangle row). Be sure to pick up both parts of slipped st; it will look like 2 sts on needle; turn.

Row 2 and all RS rows Knit to end of sts worked in previous row of triangle.

Row 3 Sl 1, p3, p2tog; turn.

Row 5 Sl 1, p2, p2tog; turn.

Row 7 Sl 1, p1, p2tog; turn.

Row 9 Sl 1, p2 tog; turn.

Row 11 P2tog.

Left-slanting rectangles (when RS is facing)

Row 1 (RS) With RS facing, pick up and knit 6 sts along the slipped selvage sts from the right-slanting rectangle or right-edge triangle. For the first rectangle only, sl the first st (the last st rem from the right edge triangle) to RH needle, then pick up and knit 5 more sts. Sl last st picked up back to LH needle and ssk; turn.

Row 2 P6; turn.

Row 3 Sl 1, k 4, ssk; turn.

Rows 4–11 Rep rows 2 and 3 four times more; after row 11 *do not turn.* Work 2 more rectangles. Rep A–D 9 times more, then work A, B and C, placing last st from right-edge triangle on crochet hook.

*Insert hook through slipped edge st, yo hook, then pull hook through both the slipped st edge and st on hook; rep from * 4 times more down slipped st edge of right-edge triangle. Using the crochet hook like a knitting needle, bind off 6 sts on needle, then crochet 6 sts down edge of right-slanting rectangle (same as triangle). Bind off 6 sts on needle, crochet 6 sts down edge of next rectangle, then bind off rem 6 sts on left-dge triangle. Cut yarn, leaving 6"/15cm tail, pull through last loop. Weave in ends. Piece should measure approx 7" x 23"/18cm x 58.5cm (from cast-on edge to tip of last rectangle).

I-Cord Strap

With dpns, cast on 4 sts, leaving a long tail for sewing. Work in I-cord as foll:

*Next row (RS)** With 2nd dpn, k4, *do not turn.* Slide sts back to beg of needle to work next row from RS; rep from * for 77"/195.5cm. Bind off. Cut yarn, leaving a long tail for sewing

Finishing

Fold the bag in the middle of the 5th side edge triangles from cast-on edge. Using mattress stitch (see page 141) sew the sides together matching up the 2 halves of the 5th triangle, the 4th triangle with the 6th, the 3rd with the 7th, the 2nd with the 8th and the first edge triangle with the 9th. Leave last 2 triangles unsewn for flap. Sew opposite side. Sew one end of strap inside side seam of bag. Taking care not to twist strap, sew opposite end of strap to opposite inside side seam.

Felting

Place bag in a lingerie bag or pillowcase. Place bag in a top-loading washing machine with soap and hot water. Add old towels to increase agitation. Stop and check bag from time to time. When size is achieved, remove from washer. Rinse in tepid water. After rinsing, place bag in a container filled with ½ gallon of tepid water and a tablespoon of white vinegar. Leave in solution for 10 minutes; rinse in tepid water. Roll up bag in a large towel and squeeze to remove excess water. Block to finished measurements, pinning points into shape. ∎

Patchwork Pillow

Patchwork Pillow

Staggered blocks of color create a modern take on patchwork in this eye-catching pillow.

Designed by Carol J. Sulcoski

Skill Level: ■■■□

Materials

- 1 1¾oz/50g skein (approx 110 yd/100m) of Noro *Kureyon* (wool) each in #102 pink/yellow/blue/red (MC), #256 pink/orange/teal (A), #264 pink/lilac/brown/purple (B) and #95 lime/hot pink/orange (C)
- One pair size 8 (5mm) needles OR SIZE TO OBTAIN GAUGE
- 17" x 17"/43cm x 43cm square of medium-weight cotton fabric (for backing)
- 16"/41cm square knife-edge pillow form
- Matching sewing thread
- Sewing needle
- Sewing machine

Size

Instructions are written for one size.

Knitted Measurements

Approx 16" x 16"/40.5cm x 40.5cm

Gauge

17 sts and 26 rows to 4"/10cm over St st (k on RS, p on WS) using size 10 (6mm) needles. TAKE TIME TO CHECK GAUGE.

Note

Roll MC into 2 equal-size balls. Start one ball from one end of the skein (MC1) and the other ball from the opposite end (MC2).

Pillow Front

With MC1, cast on 68 sts. K 1 row, then p 1 row.

Stripe 1
Row 1 (RS) With MC1, k28; with A, k28; with MC2, k12.
Row 2 With MC2, p12; with A, p28; with MC1, p28.
Rep these 2 rows 6 more times.

Stripe 2
Row 1 (RS) With B, k18; with A, k28; with MC1, k22.
Row 2 With MC1, p22; with A, p28; with B, p18.
Rep these 2 rows 6 more times.

Stripe 3
Row 1 (RS) With A, k12; with MC1, k28; with B, k28.
Row 2 With B, p28; with MC1, p28; with A, p12.
Rep these 2 rows 6 more times.

Stripe 4
Row 1 (RS) With B, k28; with A, k28; with MC1, k12.
Row 2 With MC1, p12; with A, p28; with B, p28.
Rep these 2 rows 6 more times.

Stripe 5
Row 1 (RS) With MC1, k18; with C, k28; with MC2, k22.
Row 2 With MC2, p22; with C, p28; with MC1, p18.
Rep these 2 rows 6 more times.

Stripe 6
Row 1 (RS) With MC1, k12; with C, k28; with A, k28.
Row 2 With A, p28; with C, p28; with MC1, p12.
Rep these 2 rows 6 more times.

Stripe 7
Row 1 (RS) With MC1, k28; with B, k28; with MC2, k12.
Row 2 With MC2, p12; with B, p28; with MC1, p28.
Rep these 2 rows 6 more times. With MC1, k 1 row, then p 1 row. Bind off knitwise.

Finishing

Block piece lightly to measurements. With RS together, center pillow front over fabric backing; pin in place. Machine-stitch pieces together, 1 st (or row) from the edge, leaving a 6"/15cm opening at center bottom. Clip fabric corners only. Turn RS out. Insert pillow form. Slip stitch opening closed. ■

Eyelet Bobble Scarf

Eyelet Bobble Scarf

Bobbles border a simple lace pattern, creating a fringed effect. Wear it to your next fiesta!

Designed by Halleh Tehranifar

Skill Level: ■■■□

Materials
- 5 1¾oz/50g skeins (each approx 110 yd/100m) of Noro *Kureyon* (wool) in #170 blue/pink/yellow multi
- One pair size 10 (6mm) needles OR SIZE TO OBTAIN GAUGE
- Spare size 10 (6mm) needle
- Cable needle (cn)
- Stitch markers

Size
Instructions are written for one size.

Knitted Measurements
Width (at widest point) approx 11"/28cm
Width (at narrowest point) approx 6½"/16.5cm
Length approx 73"/185.5cm

Gauge
18 sts and 20 rows to 4"/10cm over chart pat using size 10 (6mm) needles. TAKE TIME TO CHECK GAUGE.

Note
Scarf is made in two panels, then joined in the center using 3-needle bind-off.

Stitch Glossary
2-st RC Sl 1 st to cn and hold to *back*, k1, k1 from cn.
2-st LC Sl 1 st to cn and hold to *front*, k1, k1 from cn.
Make Bobble In same st work k1, [p1, k1] twice, making 5 sts from one; turn. P5, turn. K5, turn. P5, turn. Working one stitch at a time, pass 5th st on LH needle over first st on LH needle, then 4th st, 3rd st, then 2nd st over first st.

Panel (make 2)
Cast on 51 sts.
Beg Chart Pat
Row 1 (RS) Work first 5 sts, pm, work next 41 sts, pm, work last 5 sts. Slipping markers every row, cont to foll chart in this way to row 16, then rep rows 1–16 twice more.

Next (dec) row (RS) P1, 2-st RC, p2, sl marker, k1, [ssk] 6 times, k15, [k2tog] 6 times, k1, sl marker, p2, 2-st LC, p1—39 sts.
Next row K1, p2, k2, sl marker, purl to next marker, sl marker, k2, p2, k1.
Next (dec) row P1, 2-st RC, p2, sl marker, k1, [ssk] 4 times, k11, [k2tog] 4 times, k1, sl marker, p2, 2-st LC, p1—31 sts.
Next row K1, p2, k2, sl marker, purl to next marker, sl marker, k2, p2, k1.
Next (dec) row P1, 2-st RC, p2, sl marker, k5, ssk, k7, k2tog, k5, sl marker, p2, 2-st LC, p1—29 sts. Cont in rib pat as foll:
Row 1 (WS) K1, p2, k2, sl marker, [p1, k1] 9 times, p1, sl marker, k2, p2, k1.
Row 2 (RS) P1, 2-st RC, p2, sl marker, [k1, p1] 9 times, k1, sl marker, p2, 2-st LC, p1. Rep rows 1 and 2 until piece measures 36½"/92.5cm from beg, end with a WS row. Cut yarn leaving a 6"/15cm end. Leave sts on spare needle. Make 2nd panel; *do not cut yarn.*

Finishing

With RS facing, hold panels tog on two parallel needles. Using third needle, cont to work 3-needle bind-off. Block piece lightly to measurements. ■

Stitch Key

☐	Knit on RS, purl on WS	◹	P2tog
─	Purl on RS, knit on WS	◺	P2tog tbl
Ｏ	Yarn over	●	Make bobble
◹	K2tog	⋈	2-st RC
◺	Ssk	⋈	2-st LC

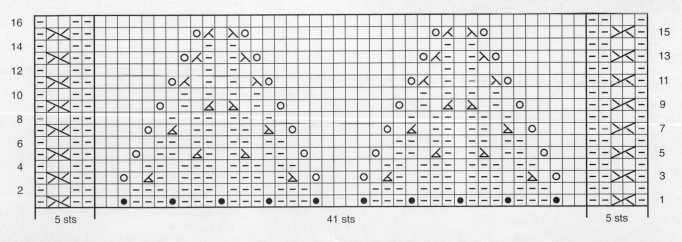

5 sts · 41 sts · 5 sts

Brioche Scarf

Brioche Scarf

The challenging stitch pattern used in this sumptuous neck warmer creates a unique color effect that is well worth the effort.

Designed by Kenny Chua

Skill Level: ■■■■

Materials

- 5 1¾oz/50g skeins (each approx 110 yd/100m) of Noro *Kureyon* (wool) in #188 moss/purple/navy
- One pair size 9 (5.5mm) needles OR SIZE TO OBTAIN GAUGE

Size

Instructions are written for one size.

Knitted Measurements

Approx 7" x 78"/18cm x 198cm

Gauge

15 sts and 32 rows to 4"/10cm over brioche st using size 9 (5.5mm) needles. TAKE TIME TO CHECK GAUGE.

Notes

1) It's important to do a swatch for gauge and to familiarize yourself with the pattern stitch.
2) When working the pattern stitch, take care to keep each loose strand created by slipping one stitch purlwise loose enough to be easily knit along with the knit stitch (on the following row), but not so loose as to take you off gauge.

Stitch Glossary

B-st (brioche st) Insert RH needle through next stitch on LH needle and under loose horizontal strand behind stitch, then knit the stitch and the loose strand together.

Brioche Stitch

(over a multiple of 2 sts)
Row 1 *Wyif, sl 1 purlwise, k1; rep from * to end.
Row 2 *Wyif, sl 1 purlwise, work B-st; rep from * to end.
Rep row 2 for brioche st.

Test Swatch

Cast on 16 sts. Work in brioche st for 32 rows. Piece should measure 4¼" x 4¼"/11cm x 11cm (including the cast-on edge).

Scarf

Cast on 26 sts loosely.

Set-up row *Wyif, sl 1 purlwise, k1; rep from * to end.

*First Triangle

Rows 1 and 2 [Wyif, sl 1 purlwise, work B-st] 12 times; turn.

Rows 3 and 4 [Wyif, sl 1 purlwise, work B-st] 11 times; turn.

Rows 5 and 6 [Wyif, sl 1 purlwise, work B-st] 10 times; turn.

Rows 7 and 8 [Wyif, sl 1 purlwise, work B-st] 9 times; turn.

Rows 9 and 10 [Wyif, sl 1 purlwise, work B-st] 8 times; turn.

Rows 11 and 12 [Wyif, sl 1 purlwise, work B-st] 7 times; turn.

Rows 13 and 14 [Wyif, sl 1 purlwise, work B-st] 6 times; turn.

Rows 15 and 16 [Wyif, sl 1 purlwise, work B-st] 5 times; turn.

Rows 17 and 18 [Wyif, sl 1 purlwise, work B-st] 4 times; turn.

Rows 19 and 20 [Wyif, sl 1 purlwise, work B-st] 3 times; turn.

Rows 21 and 22 [Wyif, sl 1 purlwise, work B-st] twice; turn.

Rows 23 and 24 Wyif, sl 1 purlwise, work B-st; turn.

Row 25 [Wyif, sl 1 purlwise, work B-st] 13 times; turn.

Second triangle

Rep rows 1–25 of first triangle*. Rep from * to * until piece measures approx 78"/198cm from beg, end with the completion of second triangle.

Last row *P1, work B-st; rep from * to end. Bind off all sts very loosely in p1, k1 rib .

Finishing

Block piece lightly to measurements. ∎

Earflap Hat

Earflap Hat

What could be cozier, or prettier, than an earflap cap knit in lace? Stitching it in soft shades of *Silk Garden Sock Yarn* puts it over the top.

Designed by Jacqueline van Dillen

Skill Level: ■■■□

Materials

- 1 3½oz/100g hank (approx 110 yd/100m) of Noro *Silk Garden Sock Yarn* (lamb's wool/silk/nylon/kid mohair) in #279 brown/blue/deep rose
- One pair size 4 (3.5mm) needles OR SIZE TO OBTAIN GAUGE
- Size F/5 (3.75mm) crochet hook

Size

Instructions are written for one size.

Knitted Measurements

Head circumference 18½"/47cm (unstretched)
Depth to front edge 8"/20.5cm
Depth to back edge 11½"/29cm

Gauge

23 sts and 35 rows to 4"/10cm over chart pat I using size 4 (3.5mm) needles. TAKE TIME TO CHECK GAUGE.

Note

Hat is made back and forth in one piece.

P2, K2 Rib

(over a multiple of 4 sts plus 2)
Row 1 (RS) P2, *k2, p2; rep from * to end.
Row 2 K2, *p2, k2; rep from * to end.
Rep rows 1 and 2 for p2, k2 rib.

Hat

Back
Beg at back bottom edge, cast on 62 sts. Work in p2, k2 rib for 10 rows, dec 1 st in center of last row and end with a WS row—61 sts.
Beg chart pat I
Row 1 (RS) Work first st, then work 12-st rep 5 times. Cont to foll chart in this way to row 10, then rep rows 1–10 twice more.
Front
Row 1 (RS) Work first st, work 12-st rep 5 times, then cast on 48 sts—109 sts.
Row 2 Work 12-st rep 9 times, then work last st. Cont to foll chart in this way to row 10, then rep rows 1–10 four times more.
Crown shaping
Beg chart pat II
Row 1 (RS) Work first st, work 12-st rep 9 times. Cont to foll chart in

this way to row 12—19 sts. Cut yarn leaving an 18"/46cm tail and thread through rem sts. Pull tog tightly, secure end, then sew seam.

Finishing
Front ribbed band
With RS facing, pick up and k 24 sts evenly spaced along right back side edge, 46 sts along front edge, then 24 sts along left back side edge—94 sts. Beg with row 2, cont in p2, k2 rib for 9 rows. Bind off in rib.

Tassel tie (make 2)
With crochet hook and 2 strands of yarn held tog, crochet a 5½"/14cm long chain. Fasten off leaving long tails for sewing. Make a 4"/10cm long tassel. Sew one end of tie to top of tassel and opposite end to bottom corner of ribbed band. ∎

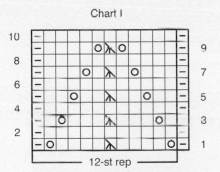

Chart I

12-st rep

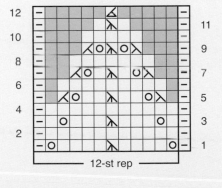

Chart II

12-st rep

Stitch Key

□	Knit on RS, purl on WS	⋌	SK2P
−	Purl on RS, knit on WS	⋋	P2tog
⋌	K2tog	○	Yarn over
⋋	Ssk	▨	No stitch

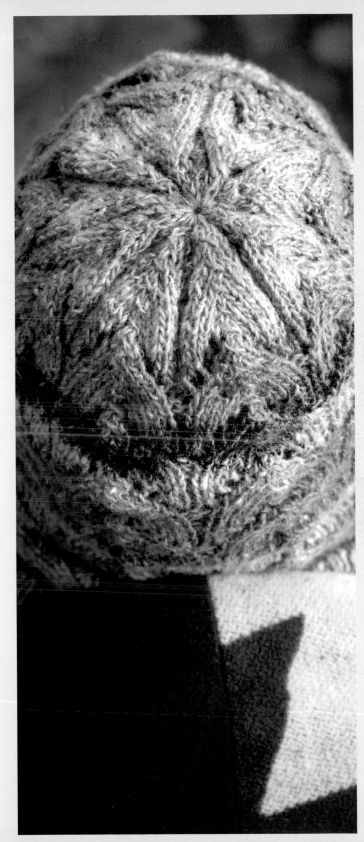

Leaves and Cables Pillow

(Continued from page 48)

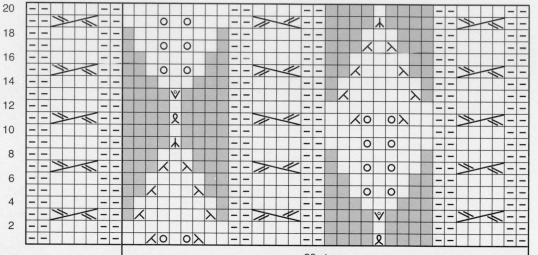

— 26-st rep —

Stitch Key

☐	Knit on RS, purl on WS
−	Purl on RS, knit on WS
O	Yarn over
⟋	K2tog
⟍	Ssk
⅄	S2KP
ⱴ	(K1, yo, k1) in same st
ⱷ	K1 tbl
⤬⤬	4-st RC
⤬⤬	4-st LC
▨	No stitch

Zigzag Pillow

(Continued from page 49)

Diamond-Wave Pillow

(Continued from page 50)

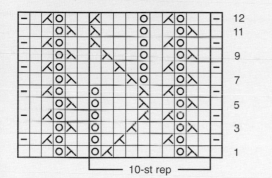

12
11
9
7
5
3
1

├── 10-st rep ──┤

Stitch Key

☐   Knit

─   Purl

○   Yarn over

⊠   K2tog

⊠   Ssk

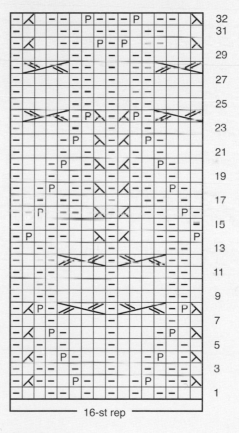

32
31
29
27
25
23
21
19
17
15
13
11
9
7
5
3
1

├── 16-st rep ──┤

Stitch Key

☐   Knit

─   Purl

⊠   K2tog

⊠   Ssk

P   M1 P-st

▱   4-st RC

▱   4-st LC

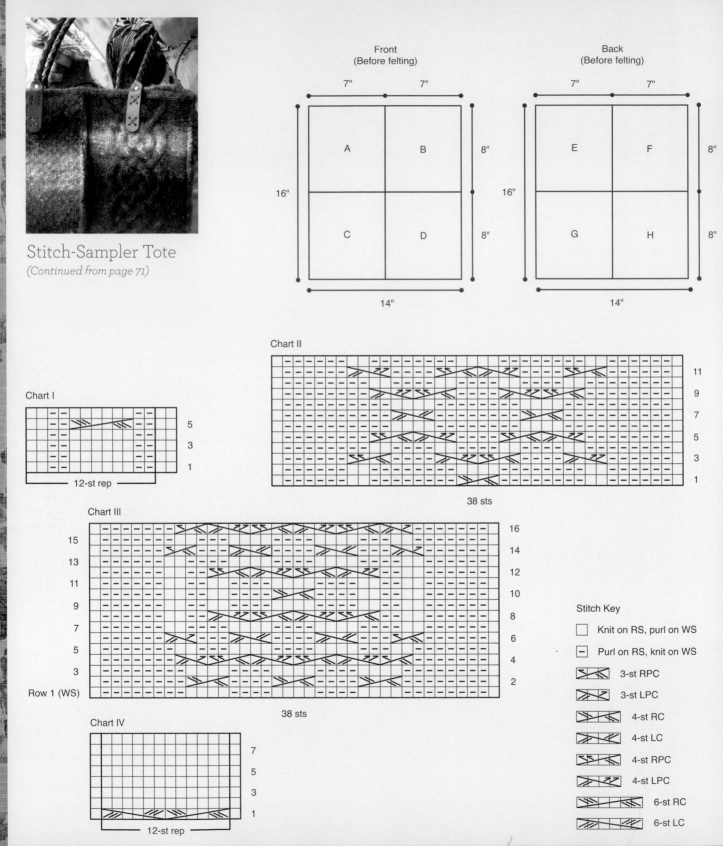

Stitch-Sampler Tote
(Continued from page 71)

Front
(Before felting)

7"   7"

| A | B |
| C | D |

16"   8"   8"

14"

Back
(Before felting)

7"   7"

| E | F |
| G | H |

16"   8"   8"

14"

Chart II

11
9
7
5
3
1

38 sts

Chart I

5
3
1

12-st rep

Chart III

15
13
11
9
7
5
3
Row 1 (WS)

16
14
12
10
8
6
4
2

38 sts

Chart IV

7
5
3
1

12-st rep

Stitch Key

☐ Knit on RS, purl on WS

− Purl on RS, knit on WS

⧅ 3-st RPC

⧄ 3-st LPC

⧅ 4-st RC

⧄ 4-st LC

⧅ 4-st RPC

⧄ 4-st LPC

⧅ 6-st RC

⧄ 6-st LC

Mitered Scarf
(Continued from page 87)

Abbreviations
CO Cast on
PU Pick up

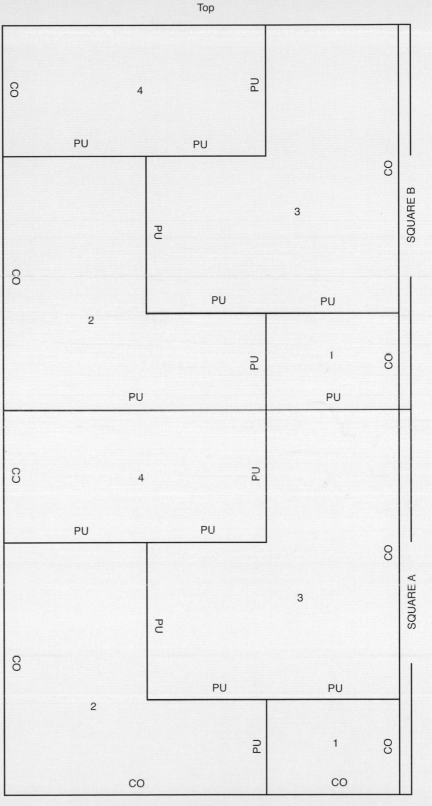

Top

CO
4
PU

PU   PU

CO
PU
3
CO   SQUARE B

2
PU   PU

PU
1
PU   CO
PU   PU

CO
4
PU

PU   PU

CO
PU
3
CO   SQUARE A

2
PU   PU

PU
1
CO
CO   CO

Bottom

Helpful Information

Abbreviations

approx	approximately	pat(s)	pattern(s)
beg	begin(ning)	pm	place marker
CC	contrasting color	psso	pass slip stitch(es) over
ch	chain	rem	remain(s)(ing)
cm	centimeter(s)	rep	repeat(s)(ing)(ed)
cn	cable needle	RH	right-hand
cont	continu(e)(ing)	rnd(s)	round(s)
dec	decreas(e)(ing)	RS	right side(s)
dpn(s)	double-pointed needle(s)	S2KP	slip 2 stitches together, knit 1, pass 2 slip stitches over knit 1
est	establish(ed)(ing)	SK2P	slip 1, knit 2 together, pass slip stitch over the knit 2 together
foll	follow(s)(ing)	SKP	slip 1, knit 1, pass slip stitch over
g	gram(s)	sl	slip
inc	increas(e)(ing)	sl st	slip stitch
k	knit	sm	slip marker
k2tog	knit 2 stitches together	ssk	slip the next 2 sts one at a time knitwise to RH needle, k these 2 sts together with LH needle
kfb	knit into front and back of stitch	ssp	slip the next 2 sts one at a time purlwise to RH needle, p these 2 sts together with LH needle
LH	left-hand	sssk	slip the next 3 sts one at a time knitwise to RH needle, k these 3 sts together with LH needle
lp(s)	loop(s)	st(s)	stitch(es)
m	meter(s)	St st	stockinette stitch
MB	make bobble	tbl	through back loop(s)
MC	main color	tog	together
mm	millimeter(s)	w&t	wrap and turn
M1	make one: with needle tip, lift strand between last stitch knit (purled) and the next stitch on the LH needle and knit (purl) into back of it	WS	wrong side(s)
		wyib	with yarn in back
		wyif	with yarn in front
M1-P	make 1 purl stitch	yd	yard(s)
oz	ounce(s)	yo	yarn over needle
p	purl	*	repeat directions following * as many times as indicated
p2tog	purl 2 stitches together	[ ]	repeat directions inside brackets as many times as indicated

Checking Your Gauge

Make a test swatch at least 4"/10cm square. If the number of stitches and rows does not correspond to the gauge given, you must change the needle size. An easy rule to follow is: To get fewer stitches to the inch/cm, use a larger needle; to get more stitches to the inch/cm, use a smaller needle. Continue to try different needle sizes until you get the same number of stitches in the gauge.

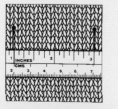

Stitches measured over 2"/5cm.

Rows measured over 2"/5cm.

Skill Levels

■□□□
Beginner
Ideal first project.

■■□□
Easy
Basic stitches, minimal shaping and simple finishing.

■■■□
Intermediate
For knitters with some experience. More intricate stitches, shaping and finishing.

■■■■
Experienced
For knitters able to work patterns with complicated shaping and finishing.

Knitting Needle Sizes

U.S.	Metric	U.S.	Metric
0	2mm	10	6mm
1	2.25mm	10½	6.5mm
2	2.75mm	11	8mm
3	3.25mm	13	9mm
4	3.5mm	15	10mm
5	3.75mm	17	12.75mm
6	4mm	19	15mm
7	4.5mm	35	19mm
8	5mm		
9	5.5mm		

Knitting Techniques

3-Needle Bind-Off

1. With the right side of the two pieces facing each other, and the needles parallel, insert a third needle knitwise into the first stitch of each needle. Wrap the yarn around the needle as if to knit.

2. Knit these two stitches together and slip them off the needles. *Knit the next two stitches together in the same way as shown.

3. Slip the first stitch on the third needle over the second stitch and off the needle. Repeat from the * in step 2 across the row until all the stitches are bound off.

Yarn Overs

Between two knit stitches Bring the yarn from the back of the work to the front between the two needles. Knit the next stitch, bringing the yarn to the back over the right-hand needle, as shown.

Between two purl stitches Leave the yarn at the front of the work. Bring the yarn to the back over the right-hand needle and to the front again, as shown. Purl the next stitch.

Mattress Stitch

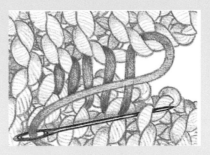

With garter stitch: Insert the yarn needle into the top loop on one side, then into the bottom loop of the corresponding stitch on the other side. Continue to alternate in this way.

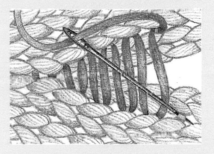

With stockinette stitch: Insert the yarn needle under the horizontal bar between the first and second stitches. Insert the needle into the corresponding bar on the other piece. Continue alternating from side to side.

Knitting Techniques (continued)

Kitchener Stitch (Grafting)

1. Insert tapestry needle purlwise (as shown) through first stitch on front needle. Pull yarn through, leaving that stitch on knitting needle.

2. Insert tapestry needle knitwise (as shown) through first stitch on back needle. Pull yarn through, leaving stitch on knitting needle.

3. Insert tapestry needle knitwise through first stitch on front needle, slip stitch off needle and insert tapestry needle purlwise (as shown) through next stitch on front needle. Pull yarn through, leaving this stitch on needle.

4. Insert tapestry needle purlwise through first stitch on back needle. Slip stitch off needle and insert tapestry needle knitwise (as shown) through next stitch on back needle. Pull yarn through, leaving this stitch on needle.

Repeat steps 3 and 4 until all stitches on both front and back needles have been grafted. Fasten off and weave in end.

I-Cord

Cast on about three to five sitches. *Knit one row. Without turning the work, slip the stitches back to the beginning of the row. Pull the yarn tightly from the end of the row. Repeat from the * as desired. Bind off.

Chain-Stitch Provisional Cast-On

With waste yarn, make a crochet chain a few stitches longer than the number of stitches to be cast on. With main yarn, pick up one stitch in the back loop of each chain. To knit from the cast-on edge, carefully unpick the chain, placing the live stitches one by one on a needle.

Distributors

To locate retailers of Noro yarns, please contact one of the following distributors:

UK & EUROPE
Designer Yarns Ltd.
Units 8–10
Newbridge Industrial Estate
Pitt Street
Keighley BD21 4PQ
UNITED KINGDOM
Tel: +44 (0)1535 664222
Fax: +44 (0)1535 664333
Email: alex@designeryarns.uk.com
www.designeryarns.uk.com

USA
Knitting Fever Inc.
315 Bayview Avenue
Amityville, New York 11701
Tel: 001 516 546 3600
Fax: 001 516 546 6871
www.knittingfever.com

CANADA
Diamond Yarn Ltd.
155 Martin Ross Avenue
Unit 3
Toronto, Ontario M3J 2L9
Tel: 001 416 736 6111
Fax: 001 416 736 6112
www.diamondyarn.com

DENMARK
Fancy Knit
Hovedvjen 71
8586 Oerum Djurs Ramten
Tel: +45 59 4621 89
Email: roenneburg@mail.dk

GERMANY / AUSTRIA / SWITZERLAND/ BELGIUM / NETHERLANDS/ LUXEMBOURG
Designer Yarns (Deutschland) GMBH
Welserstrasse 10g
D-51149 Koln
GERMANY
Tel: +49 (0) 2203 1021910
Fax: +49 (0) 2203 1023551
Email: info@designeryarns.de

SWEDEN
Hamilton Yarns
Storgatan 14
64730 Mariefred
Tel/Fax: +46 (0) 1591 2006
www.hamiltondesign.biz

FINLAND
Eiran Tukku
Makelankatu 54B
00510 Helsinki
Tel: +358 503460575
Email: maria.hellbom@eirantukku.fi

NORWAY
Viking of Norway
Bygdaveien 63
4333 Oltedal
Tel: +47 51611660
Fax: +47 51616235
Email: post@viking-garn.no
www.viking-garn.no

FRANCE
Plassard Diffusion
La Filature
71800 Varennes sous Dun
Tel: +33 (0) 385282828
Fax: +33 (0) 385282829
Email: info@laines-plassard.com

AUSTRALIA/NEW ZEALAND
Prestige Yarns Pty Ltd.
P.O. Box 39
Bulli, New South Wales 2516
AUSTRALIA
Tel: +61 24 285 6669
Email: info@prestigeyarns.com
www.prestigeyarns.com

SPAIN
Oyambre Needlework
SL Balmes, 200 At. 4
08006 Barcelona
Tel: +34 (0) 93 487 26 72
Fax: +34 (0) 93 218 6694
Email: info@oyambreonline.com

JAPAN
Eisaku Noro & Co Ltd.
55 Shimoda Ohibino Azaichou
Ichinomiya, Aichi 491 0105
Tel: +81 586 51 3113
Fax: +81 586 51 2625
Email: noro@io.ocn.ne.jp
www.eisakunoro.com

RUSSIA
Fashion Needlework
Evgenia Rodina, Ul. Nalichnaya, 27
St. Petersburg 199226
Tel: +7 (812) 928-17-39,
(812) 350 56 76, (911) 988 60 03
Email: knitting.info@gmail.com
www.fashion-rukodelie.ru

Index